# LANGUAGE TESTING

# LANGUAGE TESTING

## A Critical Survey and Practical Guide

### David Baker
*Testing Co-ordinator,*
*University of Bahrain English Language Unit*

### Edward Arnold
A division of Hodder & Stoughton
LONDON NEW YORK MELBOURNE AUCKLAND

First published in Great Britain 1989

*British Library Cataloguing in Publication Data*

Baker, David
  Language testing : a critical survey
  and practical guide
  1. Educational institutions. Students.
  Modern language skills. Assessment.
  Tests.
  I. Title
  418'.007

  ISBN 0–7131–6538–3

Photoset in Linotron Ehrhardt 10/11½pt. with Univers by
Northern Phototypesetting Company, Bolton
Printed and bound in Great Britain
for Edward Arnold, the educational academic and medical publishing
division of Hodder and Stoughton Limited, 41 Bedford Square, London
WC1B 3DQ by Richard Clay, Bungay, Suffolk

To Jone

# CONTENTS

Contents

# 1

# Making tests and making decisions

## 1.1  Shifting perspectives

The past ten years or so have seen a number of changes in the practice of language teaching. Some of these changes have been superficial, not having much effect on what teachers do in classrooms. Others have been short-lived fashions. Nevertheless it is possible to see that there has been a change in emphasis. The language teacher used to be in the business of helping the learner to master a 'system'. That is, the goals of language instruction were described in purely linguistic terms and the syllabuses which resulted were basically inventories of structural features organized in order of increasing complexity. The language teacher's task was seen as helping the learner to a gradual mastery of these features. The purposes of the language study were given little importance, since it was assumed that the structural features of the language represented an analysis at a sufficient level of generality to be applicable to all learners, from tourists to nuclear engineers. Syllabus design tended to look inward to the constituents of the language system and how they could be most effectively ordered and taught. The details of what the language would subsequently be used for were not thought to be concerns of the language teacher any more than a typing teacher should worry about what kind of text the students will have to type – learning to type begins and ends with the mastery of a well-defined set of motor skills.

Two shifts of interest occurred which changed this viewpoint. The first was the growth of interest in notional-functional syllabuses. This approach challenged the assumption that the selection and ordering of items for a syllabus should be done on purely structural grounds. It was proposed instead that the perlocutionary force of language items and their meaning relationships could be used as a basis for grouping and ordering them for teaching purposes. The effect on teaching and materials was not always as radical as was sometimes claimed: the first chapter of an elementary textbook is now called 'Introducing yourself' rather than 'The verb TO BE', but a quick glance often shows that the same structural repertoire is presented and practised as before (although items like 'Am I a man?' have probably been removed). Nevertheless, interest in 'functions and notions' did result in a shift of emphasis from the language as a hermetically sealed system towards concerns for the social and psychological dimensions of language use.

The second development which had an important effect was the growth of ESP (English for Specific Purposes). Attempts to produce courses 'tailor-made' for specific groups of learners clearly went against the idea of a single common learning process which all learners underwent. The specification of objectives for these courses contained increasing reference to the use of the language to achieve specific tasks in specific situations. The criteria of success or failure for these learners then began to be seen in terms of the performance of these tasks rather than the mastery of a linguistic system *per se.*

These shifts in emphasis in language teaching have inevitably had consequences for language testing. Testing techniques and theories, however, have been rather more resistant to change than theories about methodology and course design. This is principally because modern language testing is based on principles which, like the old 'structural' syllabuses, take as their starting point a description of the language independent of any particular use of it. The development of tests based on these principles is facilitated by a well-tried set of statistical procedures for constructing and evaluating language tests. Changes in approaches to language teaching inevitably resulted in attempts to develop testing techniques appropriate to the new pedagogy. Unfortunately, problems arise when earlier statistical techniques are extended to these texts based on more recent principles. Advocates of such tests have been forced to develop new procedures for developing and evaluating their test instruments. The legitimacy of these new techniques has been called into question.

The result of this has been to make language testing an area of considerable controversy. Such fundamental questions as 'What makes a test a good test?' and 'How should we go about constructing a test?' will receive quite different answers from adherents to different schools. Procedures acceptable to one approach may be anathema to another and so on.

Those involved with language teaching who have to make decisions about using tests can find all of this very confusing. The aim of this book is to put these issues into perspective and to give the user or writer of language tests the necessary conceptual tools to make sound, informed decisions in this field.

# 1.2 Making judgements and using jargon

There is a fair amount of specialized terminology used in talking about language testing. Often it has the effect of obscuring rather than clarifying the issues involved. We can usually avoid this by speaking plainly and using special terms with care. There is another difficulty with terminology, however, which is less easy to resolve; when a field is in a state of controversy as is the case with modern language testing, it is sometimes difficult to use terminology neutrally. Thus adopting the concepts and terminology of a particular school of testing tends to 'beg the question' when it comes to discussing the value of the procedures of that school or another.

For this reason any discussion which is intended to make sense of the issues must be conducted using terms and concepts which permit even-handed treatment of the claims and approaches of different schools. Before going on to examine in detail these different approaches to language testing, therefore, I am going to map out some common ground and introduce a few conceptual tools which will enable us to talk about each approach from as neutral a position as possible. This will involve asking basic questions about what tests are for and what kind of relationship they have to the 'real' world.

In the next chapter I shall be proposing a couple of models which should make explicit certain principles which operate in language testing. Clarifying these principles will provide a framework within which the approaches which we will examine later on can be located.

First, however, let us take a look at what testing in general is supposed to achieve.

# 1.3 Testing, decisions and procedures

Language testing is a complicated subject and much of this complication stems from problems of description and measurement which are particularly acute in linguistic and psychological investigation. It can be instructive therefore to look at other kinds of tests which do not share these particular difficulties. Life is full of tests of varying degrees of formality and important principles can often be seen operating more clearly in non-linguistic tests, where issues are simpler. Extending these principles to language testing can help to think clearly about what tests do and what they are for.

We can start by looking at two fundamental principles which provide a starting point for thinking about the goals of any kind of testing.

## 1.3.1   A test is a way of arriving at a meaningful decision

Testing is invariably associated with the making of decisions. Whenever something or someone is subjected to a test there is a decision to be made. From checking the oil level in a car to testing a baby's bathwater with the elbow, the results of the test will lead to the choice of a course of action. In the first case the motorist must decide whether to put in more oil or not. In the second case the parent must decide whether or not to put in the baby.

Langage tests also lead to decisions: a placement test, for instance, allows a school to decide in which group a learner will learn most effectively. In the case of language testing, however, this simple truth is obscured by the fact that not all language tests are tests in the real sense of the word. A familiar example is the end-of-year test in the disreputable private language school An end-of-year test should serve to decide whether the learner can pass up to the next 'level'. In certain schools, however, all learners pass to the next level whatever their performance in the first test (the school needs their fees). In this case it is easy to see that this procedure is not really a test at all since the results will change nothing. It is perhaps best regarded as a ceremony, a cathartic ritual to be undergone before the holidays. The person responsible for writing such a test can save himself a lot of the work involved in constructing a real test, since all that is necessary is that the exam be difficult and traumatic and have some vague relationship to the course the learners have followed.

A similar observation can be made about the so-called progress test. In theory a progress test can guide a teacher's decisions about his teaching or the syllabus-designer's evaluation of his programmes. Often, however, its sole purpose is as a goad to encourage regular revision on the part of the learners. Such motivating devices are useful but should not be confused with tests proper. The writer of such 'tests' will be able to write more effective motivating devices once freed from the notion that what is to be written is a test.

The 'decision' criterion can be used to decide whether testing is necessary at all in a given situation. By asking 'what decision do I need to make about these learners?', we can discover whether we need a real test, a ceremony, a goad or nothing at all. Although there is much that could be said about the construction of goads and ceremonies, what follows refers to language tests in the sense outlined above, i.e. procedures that, at least potentially, facilitate decision-making.

If we decide that we need a real test, identifying the decision that needs to be made is an important first step in constructing or choosing an appropriate instrument. If we discover that we do not need a real test, the operation of this criterion may save a lot of time and expense. Appreciation of the close link between testing and decision-making enables the test user or writer to approach the task of evaluating a group of learners with a much clearer idea of what kind of test is needed, if indeed a test is needed at all.

## 1.3.2 A test is a substitute for a more complete procedure

In the last section we were concerned with what tests are for, what purpose they serve. It was concluded that testing permits the making of decisions. We now have to look at the relationship between the economy of a test and the confidence which can be placed in its results.

Let us go back to the example of testing the oil level of a car with the dipstick. This test is quick and easy, and in general there is no reason to doubt that the level indicated faithfully reflects the volume of oil in the engine. On the other hand, the suspicious motorist always has the option of draining the oil from the engine and measuring it directly. This is much less convenient but, being more direct, eliminates any errors due to faults with the dipstick. There is a trade-off here between ease of administration of the test and the confidence which can be placed in its results. Thus a placement test consisting of an oral interview, writing tasks and various other sub-tests will be less likely to lead to misplacement than a twenty-item multiple-choice test; but it involves a lot more time and trouble.

It is possible to take this idea to an absurd extreme which, however, illustrates an important principle. If a highly sceptical motorist suspects that even draining the oil from the car does not allow him to decide whether to add oil or not (perhaps the volume stipulated in the manual is wrong), the option remains of applying the 'acid test': he can drive the car until the engine starts to complain. At that point he can be 100 per cent certain that it is time to add oil. Similarly the parent who has no faith in the 'elbow test' for the baby's bath water can put the child in and observe the results! In both of these cases, although complete confidence can be placed in the results of the procedures, there is the risk of very undesirable consequences.

It is easy to see that the dipstick and elbow tests serve as substitutes for the more extreme procedures and that we are usually prepared to forgo complete certainty in the results in return for ease of administration. This observation can be generalized to all kinds of testing: a test is always a quicker or easier substitute for a more complete decision-making procedure. This procedure can be called the **criterion procedure**. The criterion procedure is always more difficult or inconvenient than the test procedure but it is the hypothetical performance of the subject during the criterion procedure which the test procedure is designed to reveal.

This is easy to see in other examples drawn from outside language testing. Brick manufacturers, for example, have to decide whether each batch of completed bricks can be sold for building purposes, or whether adjustments need to be made to the manufacturing process. They normally take a sample of bricks from each batch and test them to destruction in a press. This is more convenient than the criterion procedure which would be to build the entire batch into a wall and observe their performance over a period of years. In spite of potential problems with the test (in this case, problems of sampling among others), the manufacturer feels justified in extrapolating from the results of the test to the hypothetical results of the criterion procedure.

Language tests also illustrate this principle. We have already seen that the function of the placement test is to decide which group of learners would be most suitable for a given student. The surefire way of placing a learner in a school (the criterion procedure), would be to put him in a class and see how he gets on, moving him if necessary. This method will eventually guarantee correct placement but is time-consuming and inconvenient. The placement test is a substitute for this criterion procedure. As anyone who has ever used a placement test knows, the results are not always satisfactory but the gain in time and convenience usually makes it preferable to the criterion procedure of letting students 'shop around' the classes. The saving in time and expense is even greater in the case of university entrance exams such as the TOEFL test in the USA or the British Council ELTS tests used by British universities. The function of these tests is to allow universities to decide if the English proficiency of a candidate is adequate for following a course of study. The criterion procedure for deciding this would be to let the candidate start a course and monitor his or her performance. Clearly, considerable time and expense would be wasted in the cases of those candidates who turned out not to be sufficiently proficient. Although the results of the tests may not permit complete confidence in decision-making (maybe the exam excludes students who could, in fact, have coped with their courses, and *vice versa*), the saving of time and money makes the risk worth taking.

Looking back over these examples, from the elbow test, through the dipstick and placement tests to university entrance exams, we can see that each is a short-cut to information about future or hypothetical performances. In each case there is a price to be paid in terms of the confidence with which extrapolations can be made. Clearly in the design of any kind of test a prime consideration must be the minimizing of this price by ensuring that the judgements which are made during the test procedure correspond as closely as possible to those that would be made during the criterion procedure. This involves ensuring that the test and criterion procedures have features in common and that these features can be adequately measured in order to arrive at a judgement. *Which* features of the criterion procedure need to be simulated in the test procedure and how they can be measured is generally much more difficult to specify with respect to language tests than other kinds of testing. In the example of brick-testing, for instance, the feature which both the testing procedure and the criterion procedure have in common is the application of a compression load to the brick. Other features of the criterion procedure (e.g. the covering of the brick with mortar) are not judged to be worth reproducing in the test situation. In constructing a university entrance examination, however, it is not so easy to identify the key features of the criterion procedure: which aspects of a student's language proficiency are crucial to future academic success is not at all clear in the absence of an adequate theoretical description. The adequacy of the test as a ground for decisions may be compromised by failure to specify these features correctly.

The extent to which a test procedure is an adequate basis for decision-making is a question of its **validity**. In the next chapter we will be addressing the problem of validity in its various aspects.

# 2

# Four models

## 2.1  Language as action vs language as system

So far we have established that tests can be used to arrive at decisions. We have not discussed exactly *how* a test may function as an aid to decision-making. In order to do this we have to look carefully at how what goes on during the test can give information about the person who is tested. Not all tests provide information in the same way. In fact we can distinguish a number of different types of language test by looking at the targets of the test and the way it is constructed. Let us start by making two distinctions:

We can distinguish between tests which take some future task as their object and those which aim to evaluate 'language' without referring to any specific use to which it might be put. We might call these **performance-referenced** and **system-referenced** tests respectively. The performance-referenced test seeks to answer questions like 'how good is this candidate at finding information in technical journals?' or 'can this candidate give simple timetable information?' The system-referenced test tries to obtain information about the candidate's ability to control certain tenses or the size of his vocabulary. What we are talking about is two ways of describing what it means to 'know' a language, the first placing emphasis on what is done with language, the second highlighting language as a code to be mastered. This distinction is not an absolute dichotomy, but rather a way of expressing opposing tendencies in test design.

The two test fragments reproduced in Figures 2.1 and 2.2 illustrate this contrast. Both are tests that involve reading texts. The first (Fig. 2.1) involves understanding instructions for using a public telephone and the second (Fig. 2.2) involves understanding a prose passage.

The first has been designed with a particular performance in mind and would give information about a candidate's ability to perform that specific task. At the same time it would be less justifiable to extrapolate from this test performance to

## Inland telephone service

### SOS – Emergency

Dial 999 to call the emergency services.
Do not insert money; these calls are free.

Fire          Police          Ambulance

### Tones

These tones indicate the progress of your dialled calls within
the United Kingdom:

### Dial tone

A continuous purring or a high pitched hum means that the
equipment is ready for you to start dialling.

### Ringing tone

A repeated burr-burr sound means that the equipment is trying
to call the number you have dialled.

### Engaged tone

A repeated single note means that the called number or the
telephone network is busy. Replace the handset and try again
a few minutes later.

### Number unobtainable tone

A steady note indicates that the called number is not in use, is
temporarily out of service or is out of order. Replace the
handset – check the number, or code and number, and try
again. If you are again unsuccessful call the Enquiry operator.

### Pay tone

Rapid pips mean that you should insert money.

---

**Remember that you may use your English–English dictionary**

*(You are advised to spend about 30 minutes on this question)*

Read the information opposite about telephone services and payphones, and then answer the
questions below.

(a)     Which tone should you wait for before beginning a call?

..................................................................................................................................

(b)     You are making a call and hear rapid pips. What should you do?

..................................................................................................................................

(c)     You are making a call and hear a repeated single note. Why isn't your call connected?

..................................................................................................................................

(d)     How much does it cost to call the fire service in an emergency?

..................................................................................................................................

Fig. 2.1

---

**Second Passage**

When she was pushed in:o the canal it wasn't the shock or the fear of drowning that worried Miranda as much as the terror of losing the letter. It was too dark to read, but she had been holding it in her hand to remind herself that it existed and that it wasn't another daydream. Her fingers held on to it even more tightly as she felt herself spinning towards the edge, but her shoulder crashed into the bridge and her whole arm went dead just before she heard the splash of her own body hitting the water.

---

51 Why was Miranda holding the letter when she was pushed?
  A She had been trying to read it
  B She had been going to post it
  C She could hardly believe it was real
  D She was very frightened of losing it

52 When she first hit the water Miranda could not have known if the letter was still in her hand because

  A she was too frightened to look
  B her hand had lost all feeling
  C the water was too dirty to see through
  D she could not remember what had happened

---

Fig 2.2

performance of other kinds of reading tasks. The second example is more general in its applicability but does not give information about any specific type of performance. This tendency to go for increased generality by limiting the domain of a test to linguistic features is typical of early work in language testing (see Chapter 3 for a discussion of this). Performance-referenced language tests, in contrast, are a more recent development. Which kind of test is more useful or appropriate will depend on the nature of the group to be tested. It is up to the user/writer of language tests to decide how generalizable the results of the test need to be and how specifically the potential or future performances can be identified. In general the most confident decisions can be made on the basis of performance-referenced tests but only if the candidates being tested share the same goals and destinations and these can be clearly specified in advance.

Cutting across this distinction is a second distinction between tests whose relationship to their object is **direct**, and those which involve a process of analysis in their construction and are therefore **indirect**.

Using the expressions introduced in the last chapter we can say that in a direct test the test procedure is very similar to the criterion procedure, whilst in an indirect test, features have been abstracted from the criterion procedure.

By way of an example, consider two ways of assessing a candidate's ability to explain how to operate a cassette recorder. The direct way is give him the machine and have him give instructions to an interlocutor. This method has the drawback of being expensive in time resources since only one candidate is tested at a time. On the other hand, if the task is performed satisfactorily, then we can be fairly sure that the candidate will be able to carry out this and related tasks in the future. The alternative method is to have the candidate write the instructions, perhaps filling in key phrases and instructions in an incomplete text. This works on the assumption that these expressions are a crucial feature of the performance and that the candidate who can use them on paper will also be able to perform satisfactorily in a 'real' situation. Time and resources are saved since we can test a whole group of people at once. The price to be paid is in the uncertainty in passing from the paper and pencil test to conclusions about 'real' performance. The reasons for preferring indirect tests, then, concern economy and ease of administration but at the cost of reduced confidence in the results.

Combining these two distinctions allows us to locate any given test on a two-dimensional grid:

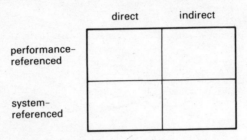

Fig 2.3

Before going on to look at these test types in detail it is worth sketching out what kind of tests fall into each category.

**Performance-referenced** language tests owe their development to the desire to have information about what a testee can actually do with his language proficiency. They are of fairly recent origin (although in the fields of vocational and professional training this approach to evaluating ability has a long pedigree and many decisions, from the certification of apprentices to the appointment of civil servants, are taken on the basis of simulation-based tests). Into the **direct** category of such tests come so-called 'communicative' tests in which the test situation is supposed to simulate as closely as possible occasions of authentic language use. The **indirect** tests aim to provide the same information, not by exactly simulating the language performance in the test but rather by breaking it down into more easily testable components. Examples include university entrance tests such as the JMB examination and British Council ELTS test.

**System-referenced** tests are older in origin. Their aim is to provide information about language proficiency in a general sense without reference to any particular use or situation.

The **direct** system-referenced test is exemplified by the very traditional testing devices of composition and oral interview when these methods are used as ways of getting a sample of language out of the candidate in order to assess its acceptability according to purely linguistic criteria such as grammaticality, vocabulary size, etc.

The **indirect** category includes most public language tests produced since the war: information is required about the testee's general language proficiency (without reference to any particular use or purpose). Rather than evoke directly a sample of language, as in the oral or composition methods, this information is acquired indirectly. Multiple-choice 'grammar' questions and vocabulary quizzes are all examples of this kind of test.

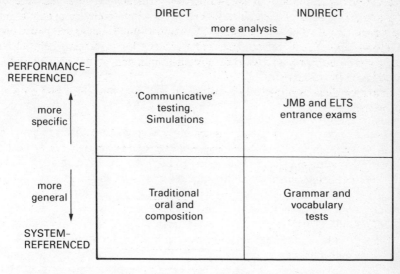

Fig 2.4

We now have to look in detail at the types of test which have been identified above. The two most important questions we will be asking about each type will be:

1 How much confidence can be placed in the results of this kind of test?
2 Exactly what line of reasoning justifies the making of decisions on the basis of such tests?

# 2.2 Performance-referenced testing

As we saw above, performance-referenced tests are a relatively recent development in language testing. We are going to deal with them first, however, since they are based on rather more straightforward principles; principles which they share, furthermore, with vocational and professional tests outside the field of language testing.

## 2.2.1 Direct testing

Let us start by distinguishing two kinds of performance:

**The test performance:**      i.e. what the testee has to do during the test
**The criterion performance:**      i.e. what the testee would have to do in a 'real' situation.

The relationship of the test performance to the criterion performance can be simply expressed as follows:

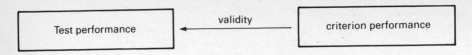

Fig 2.5

A well-known test which conforms closely to this model is the British driving test. The test performance consists of driving around and making manoeuvres for a short time. The criterion performance consists of driving around and making manoeuvres for the rest of the testee's life.

As mentioned earlier, language tests of this type are comparatively recent. Figure 2.6 shows an example from the Oxford Syndicate's preliminary test in English.

Here the criterion performance is using an English–English dictionary to resolve problems in reading. The test performance is very similar and on this basis we could be fairly confident that a candidate who performs well on the test will be able to use a dictionary of this kind effectively in the future. This illustrates a general principle of direct testing: if the test performance is sufficiently similar to the criterion performance then judgements made about the testee during the test can be considered as applicable to the criterion performance and decisions made accordingly.

Thus the driving examiner who considers that a candidate's performance during the test has been satisfactory can, with reasonable confidence, assume that his future performance will be satisfactory and therefore grant him a licence.

In discussing whether decisions can confidently be made on the basis of a test's results, we are talking, in the most general sense, about its validity. As we shall see later, several different senses and aspects of validity have been distinguished, but, following our operational definition of a test's purpose as the facilitation of decision-making, we can sketch out a basic definition in the following way: The validity of a test is the extent to which confident decisions can be made on the basis of its results.

It follows from this that the validity of a test is dependent on the purpose which it is supposed to serve. Thus a test which allows the making of one type of decision may, by this token, be invalid if its results are used as the basis of a different type of decision.

This is one way of resolving the old dispute about whether oral interviews are valid tests since shy students may do badly through no fault of their own. The usual debate on this issue revolves around whether one can separate linguistic from interpersonal skills. Approached in this way it is probably not capable of being resolved one way or the other.

If we consider, instead, the decisions that flow from the test's results then the issue is clearer: if I am selecting potential sales representatives or receptionists then the interview may be a reliable guide to the suitability of the candidates. On the other hand, if I must decide whether to reward a learner for the effort he has put into his language studies, I will have less confidence in the procedure. It should be noted that this resolution of the issue sidesteps knotty problems such as 'What is the test supposed to measure?' and 'What does it measure?' which may often be very difficult to answer. By asking instead whether the test will permit the necessary

Remember that you may use your English–English dictionary
*(You are advised to spend about 25 minutes on this question)*

5    Using the dictionary extracts, answer the following questions.

5.1   The definitions of **give** and **get** (opposite) are numbered. Put the number of the correct definition for **give** and **get** as used in the following sentences, in the space provided. The first one has been done for you.

     (a)     He has **given** himself to the cause.                     ......**8**......

     (b)     This is **getting** very difficult.                           ...............

     (c)     The girl **gave** everybody a present.                    ...............

     (d)     I'm going to keep trying to open this bottle; I'm sure it will finally **give**.    ...............

     (e)     Did you **get** that cough from your sister?                 ...............

     (f)     I just don't **get** it; I can never understand what he does.          ...............

     (g)     Did you remember to **get** that coat from the cleaner's? You promised to collect it yesterday.                                          ...............

     (h)     That music **gives** great pleasure.                       ...............

     (i)     How much did you **give** for your bicycle?                 ...............

5.2   Study these sentences and mark each one either correct (√) or incorrect (x).

---

**get**/get/ *v.* (*pres. part.* getting, *past part.* & *past tense* got /got/) **1** have something: *Nick's got blue eyes.* **2** buy or take something: *We must get some more butter.* **3** fetch someone or something: *Jenny will get the children from school.* **4** receive something: *I got a lot of presents for my birthday.* **5** catch an illness: *Sarah got mumps from her brother.* **6** understand something: *I don't get what you are saying.* **7** become: *I'm getting cold—please close the window.* **8** come or go somewhere: *When will the train get to Cambridge?* **9** make someone or something move: *Quick, get the children out of the burning house!* **get about**, go or travel to many places: *The old man doesn't get about much these days.* **get at**, be able to reach or come to a place: *I tried to pick the apple but I couldn't get at it.* **get away**, leave; escape: *Two tigers got away from the zoo last night.* **get away with**, (*a*) do something safely, which usually brings trouble: *He cheated in the exam and got away with it.* (*b*) steal or take something: *The thief got away with £5,000.* **get back**, return: *I got back from my holiday yesterday.* **get in**, come to a place: *The train got in late.* **get someone in**, ask someone to come to the house: *We got the doctor in to see our sick child.* **get into**, put clothes on: *My shoes are too small—I can't get into them.* **get off**, (*a*) leave: *We must get off at once or we'll be late.* (*b*) not be seriously punished, hurt, etc.:

*can't get my car to start.* **get together**, meet; come together in a group: *The whole family got together for Christmas.* **get up**, stand up; get out of bed: *It's time to get up, children!* **get up to.** (*a*) do something, usually bad: *I must go and see what the children are getting up to.* (*b*) come to a place in a book, etc.: *We got up to page 17 in our story today.* **have got to**, must do something: *I have got to leave soon.*

**give** /giv/ *v.* (*past part,* given /'givn/, *past tense* gave /geiv/)**1** hand something to someone: *Mother gave me a glass of milk.* **2** let someone have something: *They gave us a lovely holiday.* **3** pay money for goods: *I gave £60 for my new watch.* **4** bring a feeling, etc. to someone: *The old car is giving a lot of trouble.* **5** make or bring something: *The sun gives light and heat.* **6** send out a sound, noise, movement, etc.: *Diana gave a cry when she opened the letter.* **7** say that someone may have or do something: *I'll give you ten minutes to change.* **8** use all your time, power, etc. to do something: *Schweitzer gave his life to helping sick people.* **9** pass a sickness to someone else: *Robert gave me his cold.* **10** become weaker and less firm: *The branch of the tree gave, but it did not break.* **give someone away** (*a*) tell a secret about someone: *I'm going to hide from my brother behind the tree—please don't give me away!* (*b*) hand a bride to the bridegroom at a wedding.

Fig 2.6

decisions to be made with confidence, we can make a first rough estimate of the validity of a proposed procedure.

## Measurement and judgement

So far we have been speaking as if a direct test were merely a matter of simulating a situation which gives the candidate a chance to show what he can do. There are, however, two other aspects of the test procedure which we have not yet mentioned: **measurement** (i.e. the assigning of a score to the performance) and **judgement** (the pass/fail decision or other recommendation). These must form part of any test procedure because at the end of the day, someone must decide 'how good' the performance was and if this was 'good enough'.

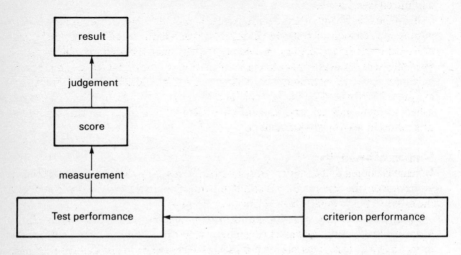

Fig 2.7

Unless the test was of an 'all or nothing' kind where nothing less than perfection is acceptable, we need some way of analysing the test performance to indicate how far it was from being perfect. In the driving test, for example, the examiner uses a checklist of sub-tasks which are ticked off as they are successfully performed by the candidate. Assessing language performance is more difficult and use is often made of a range of 'band descriptors', one of which is chosen as describing most clearly the performance being assessed, thus giving a score to the candidate. (See Chapter 6 for examples and discussion of this.)

Once the performance has been given a score, the next stage is the **judgement**, which involves deciding if the score is 'high enough'. This 'passing score' is usually decided in advance and will, of course, depend on the purpose for which the candidate is being tested. For the driving test the candidate may be allowed to perform badly on a certain number of sub-tasks without being considered a fail. The setting of this pass-mark is easier the more the test performance resembles the criterion performance. This is because it is easy to use the same criteria to judge the test performance us we would use to judge the real performance. When the two performances are rather different (i.e. the test is not very direct) it is less easy to transfer the criteria from the real situation to the test situation and it becomes less easy to stipulate how good the test performance needs to be in order to indicate a good criterion performance.

One of the advantages of the direct type of test is that it renders the setting of the pass-mark rather easier. If we consider a test which is designed to show whether a candidate could make effective notes in a lecture, a very direct test would be to require him actually to make notes from a video-recording of a lecture. The assessor could the examine the notes and decide whether they could later be used to reconstitute the content of the lecture – this being the normal criterion of adequacy in note-taking. There would, naturally, be problems in getting exact agreement among assessors about the scores for particular performances but these can be minimized (see Chapter 6).

If, on the other hand, it was decided to use a multiple-choice listening test for this purpose (i.e. an indirect test), the setting of the pass-mark would be more problematical. Although the *measurement* would be simpler, since the multiple-choice format gives the same source whoever marks it, it would be difficult to decide, just by looking at it, what constituted a satisfactory score. The normal criteria for note-taking proficiency would be inapplicable and the pass-mark would have to be established in some indirect way. Ease of measurement is achieved at the expense of difficulties in making the judgement.

### Sources of invalidity
When it is not felt that confident decisions can be made on the basis of a test then, as we have seen, the test's validity is called into question. In the case of the 'direct' test, the cause of this invalidity may be one of two things:

Firstly, the test and criterion performances may not be sufficiently similar to warrant extrapolating from one to the other, i.e. it may be doubted whether the test is in fact a direct test. This problem underlies discussions of 'authenticity' in task-based testing as we shall see later.

The second source of invalidity derives from the fact that, while life is long, tests (mercifully!) are short. It may be possible to include only a small number of features of the criterion performance in the test performance. If this part is not a representative sample of the whole performance our confidence must be weakened and the validity of the test is called into question. A driving test which only involved reversing and parking, for instance, would not be a sound basis on which to award licences.

This problem, which is usually discussed under the heading of sampling, has great importance for the kind of language tests which conform to the 'direct' model. As we have seen, the validity of this kind of test rests on the similarity between the test and criterion performance. It is the job of the test designer to set up a test situation to elicit a test performance from the candidate which will be sufficiently similar to the criterion performance. Some types of performance are easier to elicit than others, and there is a danger that the tasks chosen will be chosen for their ease of administration rather than because they are a representative sample of the criterion performance. An example of this is the much-used examiner–candidate oral interview, which is easy to set up. It is unlikely, however, that this rather unbalanced, inquisitorial speech situation will feature in much of the candidate's future performance. Of course, adminstrative constraints may force us to adopt such procedures, but this should be done in the clear realization that the sampling of the criterion performance is imperfect.

### Sources of unreliability

Even if the test performance is a good representative sample of the criterion performance this is not sufficient to make it a satisfactory test; as we have seen, measurement and judgement are essential stages in the administration of a test and things can also go wrong at this point. The adequacy of these aspects of the test form part of what is usually called the **reliability** of the test, i.e. the *stability* of the test as a measure. Very few candidates take the same test twice, of course, but a reliable test would be expected to give comparable results on repeated administrations. Some variations between scores would be extraneous to the test (the candidate might have been particularly tired during one administration), but other variations would be due to defects in the measuring and judging procedures of the test itself. For direct tests the chief source of this kind of unreliability is the person who measures and judges. A candidate who failed a driving test in the afternoon because of his poor reversing might have passed had he taken the test in the morning when the examiner was in a better mood. In language tests similar fluctuations occur in the severity of examiners' judgements and any test which does not have an 'objective' scoring format will have less than perfect inter-scorer reliability. (Methods of minimizing such variation are discussed in Chapter 6.) The validity of the test as a basis for decision making is, of course, dependent on the adequacy of the measuring and judging stages of the procedure as well as the sampling and selection which go on when the test is being designed. In order to be valid, then, a test must also be reliable.

### Summary

So far we have been looking at tests in which there is a high degree of similarity between the test and criterion performance. We have seen that this similarity is an important part of the fundamental validity of such tests and that a rule-of-thumb definition of validity is the confidence with which we can base decisions on the results of the tests. Direct tests, in common with all other types of test, involve measurement and judgement of the candidate's performance. Measurement in direct tests tends to be problematic, while judgement is facilitated by the applicability of criteria from the 'real' performance. Inadequacy of measurement and judgement in a test contribute to unreliability which, in turn, compromises the validity of the test as a basis for decisions.

## 2.2.2  Indirect performance-referenced testing

Like the direct version, the indirect performance-referenced test looks ahead to a future or potential task which the candidate will or may have to carry out. In describing the indirect test we can again distinguish a test and a criterion performance. This time, however, the test criterion performances are not very similar. This is because the test performance has been derived from the criterion performance by a process of analysis and abstraction. Of course some kind of abstraction takes place even in the construction of a direct test: the checklist which the driving-test examiner uses represents a partial breakdown of driving activity into sub-tasks. In indirect tests, however, this process of analysis and abstraction is taken much further, and results in the candidate doing things during the test which are quite different from the kind of performance that the test is designed to give information about.

As an example of this, let us consider part of a university entrance exam for post-graduate students: the criterion performance might be doing post-graduate work in an English-medium university; the test performance is reading some sentences and putting crosses in boxes on a sheet of paper. Clearly, using the criterion we adopted for direct testing, the two performances are so different as to render the test complelely invalid on the face of it. And yet, tests corresponding to this description are used all over the world and an enormous number of decisions about university admissions are confidently made on the basis of such tests every year. Applying our 'decision' criterion developed earlier, it would seem that these tests are considered by those who design and use them to have a high degree of validity. How can this be, when the test and criterion performances are so very different?

It is clear that the relationship between the two performances is not a simple or direct one. In order to investigate the nature of this relationship we have to introduce two more expressions:

> **The criterion proficiency**: i.e. what the candidate must know or be able to do in order to produce a satisfactory criterion performance,

which in this case is to follow a course of study at an English-medium university.

> **The test proficiency**: what the candidate must know or be able to do in order to produce a satisfactory test performance,

which in this case is to put crosses in the right boxes on the paper.

How do these two constructs connect to the test and criterion performances? An illustration will help to make it clear:

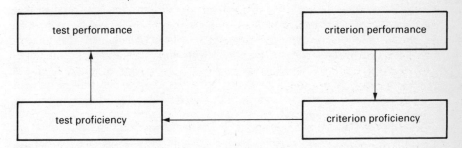

Fig 2.8

**Designing indirect performance-referenced tests**
The test designer, in making the test, follows a clockwise path starting with the criterion performance. Having made a description of the sort of things the testee will have to do (in our example, listening to lectures, making notes, asking questions, etc.) he then proceeds to identify what the candidate needs to know or be able to do in order to carry out the tasks he has described. This process of analysis can be done in a number of ways. We will be looking in later chapters at some of the ways of doing this analysis which have been proposed by test designers.

Having produced an inventory of the necessary proficiency, the test designer finds himself up against a similar kind of sampling problem to that faced by the designer of direct tests. If the analysis has been done thoroughly, the criterion proficiency will usually have many more aspects than can be dealt with in the course of an average language test. For instance, it might have been decided that a non-technical recognition vocabulary of four thousand items is necessary to follow a particular course. It is obviously out of the question to include all four thousand of these items in the test. A selection must be made. The resulting sub-set of the criterion proficiency constitutes the test proficiency. The task of the designer is now to produce a test which will indicate to what extent this proficiency is possessed by the candidate. This test must elicit from the candidate a test performance which can legitimately be considered as evidence for the specified test proficiency.

In this way, by passing in a clockwise sense round the diagram, we have established the relationship between the test and criterion performances. Not, as in the direct test, by examining the degree of similarity between them, because they are quite dissimilar, but rather, by specifying a number of procedures which, if legitimate, will permit judgements of the test performance to be extrapolated to the criterion performance.

As in the direct test, there are procedures for measuring and judging the test performance, although the problems tend to be slightly different in the case of indirect tests. We shall have more to say about this later on.

An example of an existing test which illustrates these design procedures is the ELTS test, produced by the British Council to enable British universities to assess the suitability of overseas applicants.

The stages leading to the construction of this test can be summarized as follows. (A far more detailed account can be found in Carroll, 1980.)

First the criterion performance is established by specifying which situations prospective students will find themselves in and what activities they will engage in in these situations. A very brief example of this specification for a Business Studies student is shown in Figure 2.10.

Next, the skills which the student will need in order to perform these activities are listed (in this case they are drawn from Munby, 1978). These constitute the criterion proficiency. The diagram shows a few of these which are relevant to Reference study – Intensive reading. A selection of these skills is made – the Test proficiency – and a test constructed to measure to what extent the candidate possesses these skills. A few items from the Study Skills module of the ELTS are shown in the diagram.

This account is, of necessity, oversimplified and does not touch on many of the issues and problems that this kind of project must deal with. It does however illustrate the sort of approach which is necessary to ensure the maximum validity of

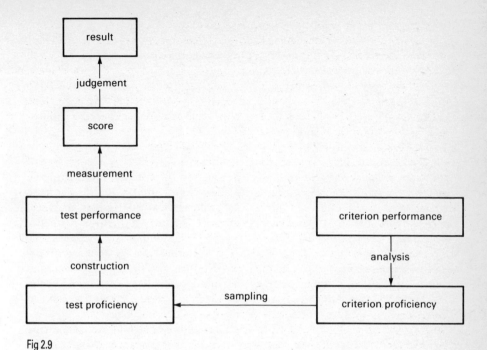

Fig 2.9

an indirect test.

## Using the test

This model can also be used to make explicit the reasoning of the test-user who is basing decisions on the test. Faced with a candidate who has scored satisfactorily on the test he starts with the test performance and proceeds anti-clockwise. Since the candidate's score was satisfactory and he believes the test to be well-constructed and properly marked he has reason to believe that the candidate possesses the test proficiency. As he believes the test proficiency to be a representative sample of the criterion proficiency he can go further and deduce that the candidate also possesses the criterion proficiency. Since he believes the criterion proficiency specification to be based on a sound analysis of the criterion performance he has reason to believe that the candidate will be capable of producing this performance. In the case of our example he can therefore offer him a place on the course.

## Sources of invalidity in indirect performance-referenced tests

One thing which is clear from the above is that our test user is having to place quite a lot of faith in several different aspects of the test procedure. Only one step in the test construction needs to be faulty for the legitimacy of reasoning from test to criterion performance to be seriously undermined. As we established earlier, the confidence with which we can base decisions on test results is a measure of the basic validity of the test. The kinds of problem which can creep in at each stage of the procedure represent, therefore, a number of sources of invalidity which may affect this kind of indirect test. Let us examine them.

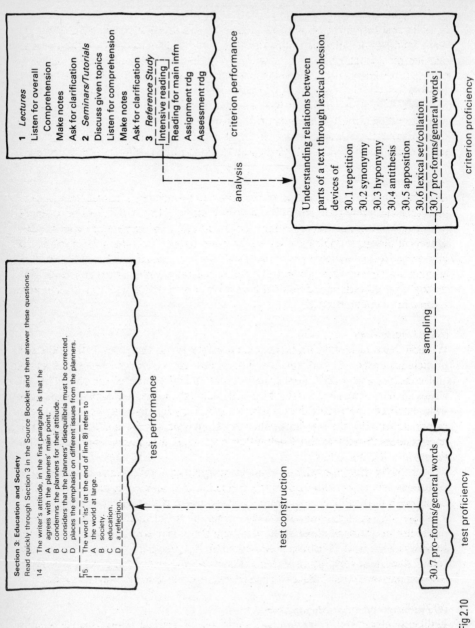

**Section 3: Education and Society**

Read quickly through Section 3 in the Source Booklet and then answer these questions.

14   The writer's attitude, in the first paragraph, is that he

    A   agrees with the planners' main point.
    B   condemns the planners for their attitude.
    C   considers that the planners' disequilibria must be corrected.
    D   places the emphasis on different issues from the planners.

15   The word 'its' (at the end of line 8) refers to

    A   the world at large.
    B   society.
    C   education.
    D   a reflection.

test performance

**1** *Lectures*
  Listen for overall
    Comprehension
  Make notes
  Ask for clarification
**2** *Seminars/Tutorials*
  Discuss given topics
  Listen for comprehension
  Make notes
  Ask for clarification
**3** *Reference Study*
  Intensive reading
  Reading for main infm
  Assignment rdg
  Assessment rdg

criterion performance

analysis

Understanding relations between
parts of a text through lexical cohesion
devices of

  30.1 repetition
  30.2 synonymy
  30.3 hyponymy
  30.4 antithesis
  30.5 apposition
  30.6 lexical set/collation
  30.7 pro-forms/general words

criterion proficiency

sampling

test construction

30.7 pro-forms/general words

test proficiency

Fig 2.10

## (a) Faulty analysis

In criticizing a given test it may be questioned whether the criterion proficiency is really an adequate analysis of the knowledge and skills necessary for the criterion performance. In other words the legitimacy of the passage from criterion performance to proficiency may be placed in doubt. It may be criticized as incomplete as, for instance, a university entrance test based solely on knowledge of vocabulary. Alternatively the whole basis of the analysis may be called into question and it may seriously be doubted whether the analysis of the criterion performance can legitimately be carried out in the terms proposed. In traditional testing terminology, the satisfactoriness of this analysis is usually discussed under the heading of 'construct validity'.

## (b) Bad sampling

Assuming that our specification of the criterion proficiency is satisfactory, we still have to decide which parts of it will form the content of the test. The same sampling problems arise as for direct testing, accompanied by the same temptations: some aspects of the criterion proficiency will be easier to test than others. It is very easy to take as our test proficiency only those aspects which will give us fewer problems of administration, even though they may not be a good sample. The road to mediocre testing is paved with bad samples. This aspect of the test's adequacy is traditionally termed its 'content validity'.

## (c) Bad construction

We now have to look at problems which may arise in the passage from the test proficiency to the test performance. This is the last stage in the design procedure and concerns the practical construction and administration of the test. The test writer's job is to produce a task which will enable the testee to demonstrate if, or to what extent, he possesses the test proficiency. Clearly, anything which prevents a candidate who has the relevant proficiency from producing a satisfactory performance renders the test invalid. Such influences include bad instructions, insufficient time and 'trick' questions.

Conversely, anything which permits a satisfactory performance by a candidate who does not possess the relevant proficiency also makes the test invalid. This category includes all kinds of cheating and things which facilitate guessing.

These problems, together with inadequacies in the measurement and judgement of the test performance (examined in the next section) constitute sources of **unreliability**. That is, they introduce variations in the results of the test which do not reflect the candidate's test proficiency. As in the direct test, the unreliability of the test as a measure compromises its use for decision-making and thus its validity.

## (d) Faulty measurement and judgement

Unlike the direct test, where it may be difficult to measure a performance reliably, this is rarely a problem in indirect tests. The analysis of the criterion performance permits the construction of a test which consists of a number of sub-tasks and items, and the result of the test can usually be expressed numerically without any trouble. Where the test consists of closed or 'objective' item-types (such as multiple-choice), variations due to inter-scorer unreliability can be eliminated. The problem with indirect tests lies in the making of the judgement. What is the pass-mark? What percentage of success in performing the test tasks would indicate a satisfactory performance in the criterion situation? Mere inspection of the test is not usually sufficient to decide this for the reason mentioned earlier: the test performance is too dissimilar to the criterion performance for the assessor to extrapolate easily from one to the other. The consequences of an incorrect setting of the pass-mark are obvious: either candidates are rejected who, in fact, possess the criterion proficiency, or candidates pass although they will not be capable of the criterion performance.

Thus we can see that there are quite a lot of factors that can seriously affect an indirect test at each of the stages of its construction and use. In practice, the last two stages of proficiency sampling and test construction can usually be accomplished satisfactorily by the use of commonsense techniques. It is the first step, that of specifying the criterion proficiency, which is the most problematical. To be fully adequate this analysis would have to make use of a comprehensive account of what using a second language in a specific context involves. No such account currently exists, even on the distant horizon. In the meantime, indirect testing must make use of such accounts as are available. It has been argued (Carroll, 1980, 14) that direct testing (where no analysis is attempted and we pass straight from criterion to test performance), is more likely to lead to truly 'scientific' tests. This debate will be taken up again in a later chapter.

**Empirical validation**
Given the problems of establishing the validity of an 'indirect' test through inspection of the design procedures, it is scarcely surprising that other methods have been developed. One important technique is to administer the test to a population together with another test whose validity has already been established. (This second test may lie closer to the criterion procedure than the one being validated.) The results of the two tests are then compared by statistical means. If the performance on the two tests is sufficiently similar, then the new test can be said to have been 'validated' by means of the old one.

For example: a university wishes to use a general English test to select overseas research students as teaching assistants. The test is easy to administer but it is impossible to see by looking at it if it is can be used to appoint teaching assistants or not. In order to establish this, another test is constructed involving videoed interviews, student questionnaires and other expensive and time-consuming procedures (the test performance on this test is much closer to the criterion performance i.e. it is a more direct test). A group of candidates is given both this test and the quick test. Statistical techniques are used to check that the two tests are 'sorting-out' the candidates in the same way. If all goes well, the quick test can be used as an economic way of screening applicants. The problem of stipulating the pass-mark can be solved in this way, too: candidates who were borderline on the elaborate test will have scores on the quick test which may also be considered borderline. In this way an approximate pass-mark can be established. (The actual techniques used, and their legitimacy, will be examined in greater detail in Chapter 4.)

In this example the validating test was especially written for the population concerned, and, being a direct test, its validity could be established by inspection. Frequently, however, a test is validated with reference to another existing, established test.

Certain objections can be raised to this procedure, however. Firstly, if the validity of the test used for validation has itself been established by reference to another test, then there is the danger of creating a collection of tests, all valid among themselves but without any connection with an external criterion. Secondly, if the development of the new test has been along different lines from that of the old test or it is going to be used with a different type of candidate, then it is doubtful whether it is appropriate to validate one against the other.

The procedure can only really be justified if it used to validate a 'quick and easy' test against a more elaborate test whose validity has itself been established by reference to an external criterion and whose purpose and target population are similar to those of the test being validated.

## 2.3 System-referenced tests

So far we have been looking at tests which aim to predict how well the candidate will perform some kind of future task. System-referenced tests, in contrast, are constructed to measure the candidate's mastery of the language as a 'system' without reference to any specific use which may be made of it. 'Language' viewed like this is a bit like 'intelligence': an unobservable entity which can be measured independently of, and without reference to, any particular employment of it; something which exists 'in the head' of the candidate underlying and facilitating certain types of behaviour.

Tests which fall into this category include most public language examinations produced in Britain and the United States since the war. Familiar examples are the examinations produced by the Cambridge Syndicate: the Proficiency and First Certificate examinations (although it should be said that some parts of these examinations reveal a shift towards more performance-referenced approaches in recent years), and the American TOEFL test. The wide currency enjoyed by these examinations is, in part, due to the decision to make them generalized system-referenced tests, rather than basing them on a more specific performance specification.

Approaching the testing of language in this way has one important advantage and one serious drawback. Since tests of this kind are oriented towards generalized mastery of the language they can be used with candidates who expect to use the language for a wide range of (possibly as yet unspecified) purposes. For this reason, a system-referenced test (such as the Cambridge First Certificate), can be chosen as the exit test for a course whose participants have a variety of goals and objectives. It may be more appropriate to have information about the attainment of these learners in purely linguistic terms rather than in relation to their ability to perform a number of specific tasks. On the other hand, decisions made on the basis of the results will be less secure since, whatever the testee is going to have to do in the future, the test has not been designed with that purpose in mind. Both of these considerations will be looked at in more detail later.

As in the case of performance-referenced tests we can make a distinction on the basis of whether the test construction involves a stage of analysis or whether the test performance is more directly related to the object of the test.

## 2.3.1 Direct system-referenced tests

If the relationship is direct then the test will take the form of eliciting samples of language from the candidate and deciding 'how much' language he knows on the basis of these samples. In this sort of procedure we can recognize the traditional testing techniques of composition, oral interview and translation. 'Traditional' because, until the advent of more systematic procedures, these were the sole means of assessing a language learner's proficiency. That is not to say that the techniques as such have no place in modern language testing; many carefully constructed tests make use of one or more of these methods. What distinguishes the *traditional* use of such devices is that the interview or the composition is treated merely as a means of getting a sample of language out of the candidate which can then be assessed on purely linguistic grounds – e.g. for grammaticality or vocabulary size. Other dimensions of the candidate's performance, such as the success with which his linguistic resources have been mobilized to perform the task of the interview or composition, are not taken into account (as they are in the performance-referenced parts of the ELTS tests for example: see Chapter 6).

As a basis for decision-making, these traditional devices have a double drawback: being system-referenced they do not permit easy extrapolation to future performances. Being direct tests they suffer from the same difficulties with measurement of the test performance as performance-referenced tests (see 2.2.2). On the other hand, their ease of administration and versatility still assure them a place in many academic testing contexts.

## 2.3.2 Indirect system-referenced tests

We now come to the most familiar category of modern language test. This kind of test aims to provide evidence about the testee's mastery of a language in a general sense by getting him to do something which is only indirectly related to language. The model is similar to that for indirect performance-referenced except that the 'language' now replaces the criterion performance as the target of the test.

### Test construction

As in the performance-referenced test, the test designer starts by analysing the target of the test which is the language. He arrives in this way at an explicit designation of what 'knowing' the language consists of. This can be done in various ways and the kind of categories which are often used are familiar: pronunciation, vocabulary, listening, etc. Figure 2.12 shows the way in which language proficiency is broken down for the purposes of the Cambridge First Certificate.

It can be seen that the candidate's proficiency is broadly classified into Reading, Listening, Oral and Writing skills, and a generalized knowledge of structural matters, termed Use of English. Each one of these areas is probed by means of a separate 'paper' containing a number of sub-tests derived from a further analysis of that proficiency area. Thus the reading skill is considered to have as an important dimension, the learner's recognition vocabulary. A sample of this vocabulary is chosen and a sub-test written to assess the candidate's mastery of this sample. In the next chapter we shall be looking in detail at 'structuralist' linguistic theories which

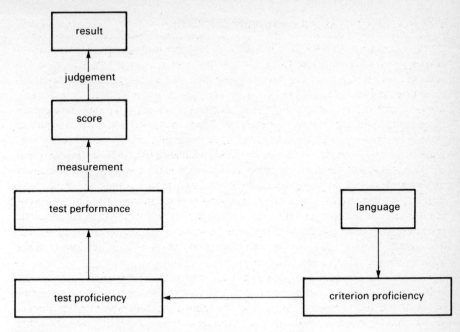

Fig 2.11

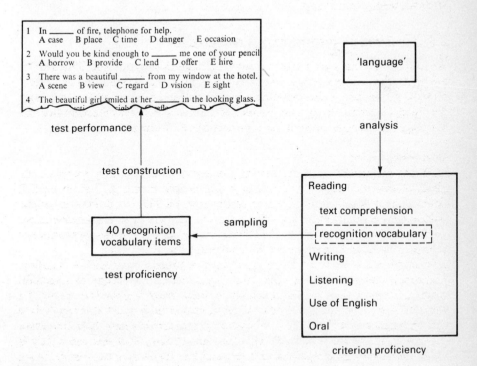

Fig 2.12

have been by far the most influential approach to this analysis.

We can see that this process of test construction follows the same path as the performance-referenced test: a representative sample of the criterion proficiency is chosen as the test proficiency and tests are constructed to probe the extent to which the testee possesses this sample. Since the test is an indirect one the best perform-ance may consist of very un-language-like behaviour indeed – putting crosses in boxes, writing single words in spaces, etc. This kind of format can be found in most language tests written since the war.

### Using the indirect test

What can the user do with the results of a test like this? Let us follow his chain of reasoning round the model. If the result is a pass then he deduces that the candidate possesses the test proficiency to a satisfactory degree. Since this is representative sample of the criterion proficiency, the chances are good that he possesses that as well. If he believes that the criterion proficiency is derived from a satisfactory analysis of the language he can conclude that the candidate knows 'enough' of the language. Enough of the language for what? we might ask. And it is at this point that the advantages and limitations of the system-referenced test reveal themselves: if the user wants to know what a given result means it is up to him to make the connection between test score and specific performance. This specification is not built in to the test. The user can make this connection informally ('The last bilingual secretary I had with this certificate coped very well') or an empirical validation study can be carried out to establish what test scores are necessary to perform successfully in given situations. We should not, however, expect very trustworthy indications about future performances from a test which was not constructed with such per-formances in mind.

This lack of specificity, however, is also one of the test's strong points: not being specially relevant to any particular candidate or purpose, it is vaguely relevant to all and therefore lends itself to use where future language use cannot be specified, or varies a lot among the candidates.

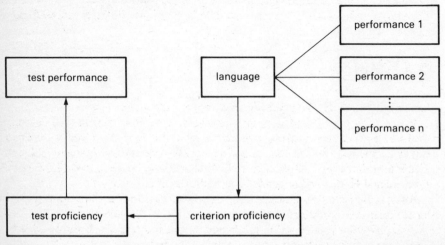

Fig 2.13

**Sources of invalidity**

Similar considerations apply to the validity of these tests as to the performance-referenced indirect tests; the analysis, sampling and construction stages must be all carried out satisfactorily for the user to trust the test as a source of information about the candidate's mastery of the language concerned. Similar problems and temptations arise at each stage. The analysis which is used to derive the criterion proficiency from 'the language' may be criticized as incomplete or based on an inadequate linguistic description. In selecting a sample as the test proficiency the test designer may have succumbed to the temptation of giving more emphasis to features which are easy to test, such as receptive skills, while neglecting aspects which can only be probed using difficult-to-administer oral tests. Finally, the actual putting together of the test may not ensure that the test performance properly reflects the test proficiency because of badly designed questions or cheating, etc.

Exactly the same considerations concerning measurement and judgement of the test performance are applicable here as in the performance-referenced test. The use of closed question types such as multiple-choice mean that the scoring of the test may be done reliably. The problem lies in the judgement. We have seen (2.2.2) that extrapolation from an indirect test score to a future performance is difficult and has to be done informally or by a empirical validation. In the case of the system-referenced test the problem is rendered doubly difficult. Since the candidates of this kind of test do not share future goals, the pass-mark has to be established independently of any considerations of 'fitness for future performance'. What can such a pass-mark mean? Well, in the case of a public examination which has achieved general currency such as the Cambridge First Certificate, the objective may be to establish a standard which represents a certain level of mastery of the language, without making any explicit claim as to what a learner holding the certificate can or cannot do. Such a standard, if it gains general acceptance, can then be used as a basis for decision-making by educators and employers who have established informally what it means. The task of the examining body is then to maintain the stability of the examination by ensuring that a pass in any one administration corresponds to the 'same' level of proficiency as a pass in previous or subsequent administrations. How this can be done leads to discussions of norm-referencing which will be dealt with in detail in Chapter 3.

# 2.4 Resumé

Let us briefly sum up the points that have been made so far.

It has been established that the purpose of tests is to permit well-informed decisions and that a consideration of the decisions that a test must facilitate is a good way to decide if a test is needed and, if so, of what kind. We have also seen that the extent to which a test will allow confident decisions to be made is a measure of its fundamental validity and depends both on the test and its purpose.

A test is always a substitute for a more complete procedure whose validity would be maximal and represents a point of reference for the test-writer.

This 'criterion procedure' is the hypothetical ideal test which would elicit the 'criterion performance' which the testee must produce in the 'real world'.

A classification of test types can be made on the basis of the target of the test and its relationship to it. When the test is constructed to allow extrapolation from its result to some specific performance it may be called **performance-referenced**. When the test's target is uncontextualized language mastery it may be called **system-referenced**.

The construction of a test may be **direct** in that the test performance is very similar to the target of the test. Alternatively it may be **indirect** and involve analysis of the target into components.

In a performance-referenced test, the test performance gives evidence about the quality of the future or potential criterion performance. When the two performances are similar the test is of the 'direct' type and if they are sufficiently similar, legitimate inferences are possible about the criterion performance on the basis of the test performance. Measurement of the test performance may be difficult because its complexity may make it difficult to choose the essential features to be assessed.

If the two performances are not similar the test is of the 'indirect' type. In this type of test the criterion performance is related to the test performance via two theoretical constructs: the criterion and test proficiencies. Inferences about the criterion performance on the basis of the test performance are legitimate only if each link of the chain of procedures relating them is satisfactory.

Of these links, that involving the derivation of the criterion proficiency from the criterion performance is usually the most unsatisfactory due to the lack of an adequate framework for analysing language situations. Owing to the difficulty of establishing the validity of this kind of test through its design sequence, this may be done statistically with reference to another test providing the two are sufficiently similar. Measurement of the performance in this kind of test is usually easy since the analysis will have broken it down into components. Deciding on the 'pass-mark' is, however, made more difficult by the great difference between the test and criterion performances.

In a system-referenced test, the test score gives evidence about the testee's mastery of the language in a general sense. Traditional testing devices like composition and oral interviews are direct system-referenced tests and suffer from several defects. Most post-war language tests are of the indirect system-referenced type. Although they may be valid in a number of senses, decisions based on their results are rendered problematical by the need to extrapolate from language score to performance. They have the advantage, however, of wide applicability.

# 2.5  Application of the models

We have been looking at testing in quite abstract terms and it would be a mistake to suggest that all language tests can be slotted neatly into the categories above. One quite often finds a range of degrees of 'directness' among the sub-tests which go to make up an exam. Sometimes performance and system-referenced formats may be found together in the same test. Nevertheless, the models which we have established will help us to put into perspective the different tendencies in testing which we are going to examine. In particular they will allow us to see more clearly the principles which, often not explicitly, underlie each approach.

# 3

# The psychometric legacy

## 3.1 The origins of modern language testing

Before the Second World War the idea of language testing as a distinct activity scarcely existed. If a learner had to be assessed for second-language proficiency this was done using the same means as had been used to teach it: composition, translation, dictation, etc. The distinction between teaching and testing was not clearly drawn.

A number of factors contributed to the development of interest in systematic 'scientific' language testing after the war. Wartime language programmes in the United States and elsewhere and the growth of international agencies gave new importance (and funds) to language teaching projects. Methods of evaluating the effectiveness of these projects were required and the work done in the United States during this period quickly became the prevailing orthodoxy in the field of language testing. It would be difficult to exaggerate the extent to which current ideas about language testing have been influenced by this approach. Virtually any discussion of the subject will make use of terms and assumptions drawn from this school, even by those who have never heard of it and might find its methods and principles quite objectionable if they had. For this reason it is important for us to examine it carefully and see exactly what its legacy has been.

The roots of the approach can be traced back to two separate academic traditions.

### 3.1.1 Psychometric testing

The 1920s and 30s saw a great vogue for psychological 'testing'. Large numbers of tests investigating every aspect of the psyche from intelligence to job aptitudes were produced and millennial predictions were sometimes made about the social benefits that large-scale testing of this kind would bring. Few of these tests actually delivered the miraculous solutions which had been promised but they survive today in the form of intelligence tests and, in a less serious form, as magazine quizzes of the kind, 'Are you a good husband?' etc.

These tests had two characteristics which were to be important for language testers. Firstly the questions were of the 'closed' type, i.e. the testee had to choose between a limited number of responses:

---

If you were at a party where you didn't know anyone, would you:

a) start a conversation with someone?
b) wait for someone to talk to you?
c) wait for someone you knew to arrive?
d) go home?

---

Fig 3.1

Secondly, a fairly elaborate system of statistical procedures had been evolved for developing and evaluating this kind of test. The first characteristic promised 'objective' scoring since whoever marked a test, the result would be the same, unlike say, marking a composition. The second characteristic offered a ready-made set of methods and criteria for analysing and evaluating language tests. For this reason, the methods and terminology of the psychological testers were adopted with enthusiasm by the those in the field of language testing. The resulting approach to evaluating language proficiency is now termed 'psychometric'. The most easily recognizable legacy of this school to present-day practice is the multiple-choice test.

## 3.1.2  Structural linguistics

The psychometric tradition in psychology provided the tools for producing and developing tests. What was also required was a basis for the *content* of the tests which were produced. What kind of thing should be tested in a language test? Here, naturally enough, use was made of the same framework that was being used to devise the teaching programmes: a language description broadly based on the work of American 'structuralist' linguists. Crudely expressed, the analysis used involved breaking the language system down into small bits, and then describing the ways in which these bits could be put back together again to make stretches of speech. The description was hierarchical in shape, the basic 'bits' being phonemes at the bottom of the pyramid which combines to produce morphemes, which combine . . . etc.

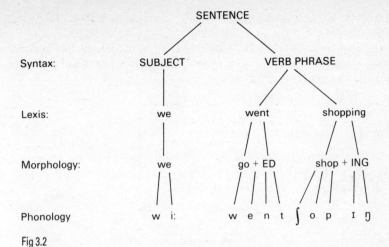

Fig 3.2

This sort of analysis looked very promising for chopping up a language into pieces for teaching and testing purposes. There was thus a close match between testing and pedagogic theory – always a desirable state of affairs. The teaching applications of this analysis were not, unfortunately, to enjoy lasting success in their original form. The audio-lingual method, as it was called, soon fell out of favour with language teachers (and students!) because of its emphasis on mechanical repetition of language elements and neglect of meaning. On the testing side, however, the approach met with little opposition and many of its categories and terms are still in use today – often ill-matched with the pedagogic approaches that succeeded the audio-lingual method. In the next section we will examine closely the way in which the analysis was tackled.

## 3.2  Details of the psychometric approach

It should be clear by now that this approach conforms quite closely to the indirect system-based testing model presented in the last chapter. Let us take a look at the model again to orientate ourselves:

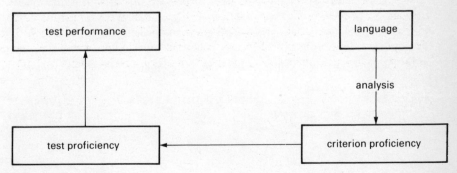

Fig 3.3

The adoption of the structuralist description constitutes the analysis which is used to derive the criterion proficiency from the language. In other words this description of language, according to the psychometric testers, provided the answer to the question 'What does the testee have to know or be able to do in order to use the language?'. The inventory provided by the analysis constitutes the description of the criterion proficiency. What exactly did it consist of?

## 3.2.1  The dimensions of proficiency

The classic statement of the approach is to be found in Robert Lado's book *Language Testing* (Lado, 1961), where, with admirable clarity, are set out the basic principles and procedures of psychometric testing.

Following the structuralist tradition, language is divided into elements at four levels:

| | |
|---|---|
| 1  Phonological: | phonemes, stress and intonation patterns |
| 2  Lexical: | vocabulary items |
| 3  Syntactic: | grammatical structures |
| 4  Cultural: | a 'dustbin' category containing what would now be called sociolinguistic and pragmatic features |

This breakdown provided the basis for listing and categorizing the 'bits' of language which were to be taught or tested. The next step was to identify the various ways in which the bits could be mobilized in actual language use. The result was the familiar 'four skills': speaking, listening, reading, writing.

We now have four categories of elements and four 'modes' in which they can be tested:

| | A Speaking | B Listening | C Reading | D Writing |
|---|---|---|---|---|
| 1 Phonology | | | | |
| 2 Syntax | | | | |
| 3 Lexis | | | | |
| 4 Culture | | | | |

Fig 3.4

(In reading and writing skills 'graphological' elements replace phonological elements.)

In theory, each square of the grid can give rise to a separate sub-test. In square B1, for example, we can locate a test of the candidate's mastery of phonology through listening:

Indicate which word you hear:

a) ship
b) chip
c) sip

Fig 3.5

Square D2 gives rise to a written grammar transformation test:

Rewrite the sentence so that it means the same.

Someone has stolen my car.

My car _____

Fig 3.6

Locating this schema on our model, it looks something like this:

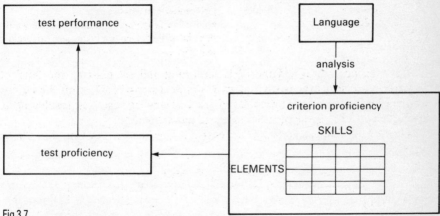

Fig 3.7

## 3.2.2  Elements vs situations

It should be clear by now that the type of tests we are dealing with are system-referenced tests *par excellence*: in deriving the elements and skills (the criterion proficiency) no mention has been made of a criterion performance. The analysis has been derived from 'The Language' as a system without reference to any use which may be made of it. This is quite explicitly defended by Lado:

> If there were a high uniformity in the occurrence and use of the various variables and units of language we could simplify the testing of a foreign language a great deal . . . This is not the case, however. The situations in which language is a medium of communication are potentially almost infinite. . . . The elements of language on the other hand are limited and it is more profitable to sample these elements than to sample the great visibility of situations in which language can be used. (1961,26)

This contention, that the situations of language use were too various to be systematically sampled for testing purposes, provided the foundation for an approach to language testing which went unchallenged for many years. Even today, as we shall see when we come to look at 'task-based' tests, there is considerable disagreement as to whether deriving language tests from specific performance requirements is feasible or worthwhile.

## 3.2.3  Discrete point 'objective' test formats

So far we have discussed the content of the tests. Now we must look at the formats which were adopted, as we mentioned earlier, from the field of psychological testing.

The kind of questions (usually termed 'items') which were used included:

> Multiple choice items
> Sentences with gaps to be filled
> Sentences to be transformed in various ways

All of these item types have the following characteristics:

> 1  There is usually only one possible correct answer for each item.
> 2  Each item samples a particular element through the use of one skill.
> 3  Items are not dependent on one another – changing one item does not change the testee's performance on the other items of the test – cf. cloze testing.

These characteristics have several important consequences for the development and administration of the test:

The 'closed' item type means that the scoring of the test need not rely on the 'subjective' judgement of the assessor, who can be a completely unqualified person. This produced obvious savings in time and expense of administration. There was a price to be paid, however, in test development costs since discrete-item tests require rather more careful development than older methods (although there are economies of scale to be achieved by centralization).

The 'specificity' characteristic allowed the claim that specific language features could be probed with great precision without the interference of other features. This claim (as we shall see later) has been somewhat eroded in recent years by demonstrations that the relationship between test proficiency and test performance is not as simple as was once believed.

The independence of items within the test permitted the changing and elimination of unsatisfactory items during the development of the test, leaving the behaviour of the other items unchanged. This was essential to the process of piloting a test using the kind of item analysis techniques which will be described in the next chapter.

A point needs to be made here about the relationship between these formats and the model which provided the test content: the adoption of one does not necessarily entail the adoption of the other. That is, the use of closed-question formats such as multiple-choice does not mean that the test writer has to embrace the view of language proficiency that the psychometric tests put forward. The following item, for example, while using a multiple-choice format, probes an area of the candidate's knowledge that would be hard to locate on the grid presented above:

```
1   "Have you got any plans for the summer?"

    You answer:
    a) I can't find them anywhere
    b) We didn't go anywhere
   *c) We're staying at home
    d) Sorry, I haven't
```

Fig 3.8

As well as lexical and syntactic knowledge, this item also requires familiarity with an idiomatic formula and understanding of its pragmatic role in conversation. The item probes knowledge of *use* rather than merely *usage*.

The multiple-choice test is often maligned; more, it seems, for its association with psychometric testing than for any intrinsic 'wickedness' it may have as a format.

Conversely it would be possible to write a question based on the model – but using a non-discrete-point format:

```
Write a short paragraph about the things you enjoy.
```

Fig 3.9

This could be guaranteed to elicit certain forms of the verb phrase, thus putting it in square D2 of our grid – testing syntax through writing. Since it has an indefinite number of answers and involves a plethora of different elements it is clearly not a discrete-point 'objective' item. The method of testing and the content of the test, then, can be separated and it is a mistake to condemn the closed-question formats of psychometric testing solely because they are traditionally associated with a rather arid and discredited view of language proficiency.

## 3.2.4 Summary

Before going on to look at the pros and cons of the approach, let us take stock of the features that we have identified so far.

We have seen that the approach had its origins after the Second World War and drew its methods and principles from two main sources. From structuralist descriptions of language it took the hierarchical analysis of language for the purpose of teaching and testing. From psychometric testing theory it borrowed the discrete-point 'objective' test formats and the statistical apparatus used for test development.

This type of test conforms closely to the system-referenced indirect model in that its object is 'language' and it uses an analytical procedure to arrive at the test proficiency.

The format of psychometric tests was designed to permit ease of administration, statistical 'tinkering' with the test, and the probing of specific language features. It was noted that adoption of such formats did not entail adoption of the linguistic model and *vice-versa*.

# 3.3 Evaluating the approach

Is the psychometric approach a 'good' way to construct language tests? It has certainly enjoyed enormous popularity and success; many important public examinations at an international level are constructed according to principles derived from the approach. It is difficult to talk about language testing without borrowing bits of its terminology. Is this success deserved? These questions are best answered by taking the model and the format separately.

## 3.3.1 The model

As a description of language, the structuralist analysis into elements and levels and its rather spartan methodology was an excellent theoretical construction. The use of such an analysis as a basis for constructing language tests was the first attempt to provide language testing practice with an explicit rationale. As such it was vastly superior to the *ad hoc* practices it replaced. Lado's exploitation of it is clear, explicit and coherent. And yet, its relevance to second-language learning is not entirely convincing. No one uses the fully-fledged analysis any more: phoneme discrimination and production, for instance, one of the most important features of the analysis, are notably absent from most modern language tests. What can we say about this?

Well, one problem is that the structuralist analysis (like most linguistic descriptions) has no time dimension: it presents a 'frozen' picture of a static system. This is fine for the normal needs of theoretical linguists, but has drawbacks when we need to describe language learning and use, activities which take place in time. In specifying a second-language learner's mastery of the system it is not sufficient to list the elements he 'knows', we must also state 'how much' mastery he has of them; to use a data-processing image, we need to describe what kind of 'access' he has to them. This involves recognizing that there is a 'real-time' dimension to language use since the poorer a learner's access to an element, the more time he will need to mobilize it in a speech situation. This is recognized informally by language teachers who are familiar with the distinction between 'teaching the language' which leads to time-constrained mastery and 'teaching *about* the language' which merely transmits passive knowledge which cannot be later accessed effectively in real-time performance.

The psychometric model goes some way towards recognizing this by specifying the modes (speaking, writing, etc.) in which the elements will be used, but the division into four skills does not accurately represent the way in which a speaker's language activities are normally grouped. By far the largest amount of most users' time is spent speaking and listening at the same time in conversational settings. This involves skills which are rather different from those required for speaking and listening separately – activities which make up a much smaller proportion of a speaker's use of language. In particular, the mobilization of isolated language elements in single-modes does not do justice to the dynamic meaning-negotiating activity which more recent work in linguistics would suggest constitutes normal language use.

As a basis for characterizing the elements and skills to be mastered, the structuralist analysis looks poor compared with the kind of descriptions of language use which have become available over the last two decades. On the theoretical side M. A. K. Halliday's Functional Grammar with its emphasis on the primarily social function of the language system provides a more subtle, if less rigorous, approach to language structure. Pedagogic advances include Munby's Communicative Syllabus Design (1978) of which an extract is reproduced in Figure 2.10. Other examples of more up-to-date analysis include the Council of Europe's Threshold specification for communicative language use (van Ek, 1975). On the other hand it could be argued that the aspects of language activity which are identified in these accounts aren't strictly language skills as such and therefore should not form part of a test of language. (This is a criticism of 'communicative' test methodology which we will look at later in Chapter 6.) In the meantime perhaps it is sufficient to note that modern tests which have their origins in the psychometric tradition tend to conform to the analysis more in the spirit than in the letter: what seems to have been preserved is a 'diluted' version of the original in which the rigid and systematic testing of elements at each level has given way to a more homely collection of categories: 'reading comprehension', 'grammar', 'vocabulary', etc. (see the Cambridge FCE specification in Figure 2.12 for an example of this). Diehard structuralist testers might claim that the loss of rigour in abandoning a strict linguistic analysis compromises the value of such tests but this is a moot point.

## 3.3.2 The instruments

In the last section we looked at the good and bad points of the structuralist approach to language analysis for testing purposes. Now we must evaluate the other aspect of the approach: discrete-item test formats. Earlier we listed some of their advantages:

> They simplify administration since they can be scored by unqualified personnel (or even by machine).
> Each item can address a distinct feature of the test proficiency.
> The test writer can 'juggle' the items within the test without worrying about the effect on the other items.

Does this mean that these formats are the answer to a test-writer's prayers? No, not entirely. There are certain drawbacks:

(1) Most of the discrete-point item types involve little or no active production on the part of the candidate. The multiple-choice format requires only that the testee *recognize* the correct form. Others require the writing of just one word:

---

No sooner _____ he arrived than everything went wrong.

---

Fig 3.10

or, at most, part of a sentence:

> Rewrite the sentence so that it means the same using the word in brackets.
>
> I last saw him in March
>
> (SINCE) _____

Fig 3.11

These types of test item are often criticized because they do not involve much production of language. This is certainly true. It should not be forgotten, however, that these are indirect test types and the items may give information about language and performance provided the construction procedures linking the item to its object are satisfactory. Thus in the second example above, if a testee provides an acceptable response we may assume that he has mastered certain structural and referential aspects of the Present Perfect tense. If we consider that the Present Perfect tense is a meaningful unit of language proficiency derived by an adequate analysis of the language, we can conclude that the candidate has mastered a significant element of the language. Our legitimate doubts here should concern not the *smallness* of the response, but rather its lack of time constraints. The ability to produce an acceptable response on paper at the candidate's leisure does not necessarily imply the ability to mobilize the same language feature within the time constraints of a normal speech situation. Surprisingly, little research has been done into the extent to which performances on paper-and-pencil tests are related to performances in more time-constrained situations. In the absence of such information we would do well to be cautious in extrapolating too readily from one to the other.

(2) A second problem involves what has been called the 'method' effect. This concerns the extent to which a candidate's performance on a multiple-choice vocabulary test, for instance, is a measure, not only of his vocabulary, but also of his ability to do multiple-choice tests. Recent research (Palmer and Bachman, 1980), while not completely conclusive, suggests that there is interaction between the 'trait' (as the proficiency feature is sometimes called) and the 'method' used to investigate it. While this research gives little indication of how great this interaction is, it serves as a warning not to treat discrete-item formats as if they were completely neutral measuring instruments.

(3) A third drawback is that since these sorts of items are quite odd as tasks, it is not easy (even for the experienced test writer), to say how difficult they are or even if they 'work' as items, just by inspecting them. For this reason the test writer must use the sorts of techniques (outlined later in this chapter and the next) for analysing and evaluating items during the development of the test and setting 'pass-marks' when the test is being used.

We can see, then, that discrete-item formats offer considerable savings in time and money during the administration and scoring of the test. There is a price to be paid, however in the increased work involved during test development and a certain indeterminacy in the interpretation of results.

# 3.4 The pass-mark problem: is norm-referencing wicked?

The kinds of test we have been looking at fall into the indirect system-referenced category. This makes it doubly difficult to interpret the results of the test and to decide if a given score is satisfactory or not. Part of this difficulty stems from the fact that the test gives information about language mastery, not future performance. As we saw earlier, this puts the onus on the test user to make the connection between exam result and future performance. The other problem is that these tests are indirect: the test performance is not very similar to normal language behaviour. This makes it quite difficult to say what the scores *mean*. In a direct test, if a candidate can chat to the examiner for a few minutes without serious breakdowns of communication, then we can say, very loosely, that he has a good basic command of the language. If instead, the candidate scores 75 per cent on a multiple-choice grammar test, it is much more difficult to say what this means, even in the most general sense. Part of the problem is that we don't know how difficult the questions in the test were.

The problem is particularly pressing if we have to make some kind of decision about the candidate (even the relatively trivial one of whether to give him a certificate). In this case we have two options: we can conduct an empirical validation against another test whose scores we *do* know the meaning of, or we can ask to have his score in another form, asking 'what percentage of the other candidates scored more than him?'. This **percentile** score will tell us how good he is relative to the group who took the test. If we know the composition of this group we are in a position to interpret the percentile score. We are more likely to be impressed if the group are all graduates in the language than if we hear that they are all recently-arrived illiterate immigrants. This illustrates the point that if we use the candidate's position within the group to estimate how 'good' his performance was (a technique called **norm-referencing**), the value of our estimate will be dependent on the overall ability of the group.

In some public exams such norm-referencing is used to set the pass mark: it is decided in advance to fail the bottom 40 per cent, say. On the face of it this seems very unfair; after all, it penalizes the candidate who happens to take the exam when the field is 'strong'. Looked at from another point of view it is a little more defensible:

Most public exams are held two or more times a year. The aim of the test writer is to keep the same level of difficulty from one year to the next. If the exam is of the indirect system-referenced type there is, as we have seen, a problem with establishing how difficult the questions are: mere inspection is not usually enough. The test-writer has a choice: he can decide that the pass-mark is always 50 per cent year in, year out. (If he happens to set a difficult exam one year then that is unfortunate for the candidates of that year.) Alternatively he can wait until he sees the results before he fixes the pass-mark so that if he has set a difficult exam he can lower the pass-mark accordingly. That is, he norm-references the exam. He does this because he believes that the ability of the population of candidates remains more stable from year to year than the difficulty of his tests. If the populations are large enough and there are no extraordinary factors, this assumption will usually be justified. Thus, the practice of norm-referencing to determine the meanings of scores, although apparently circular and incestuous, can be justified in certain circumstances.

Of course, it would be more convenient if we didn't have to have recourse to these devices to decide what a satisfactory result was, if the test result could be directly translated into meaningful terms on the basis of the candidate's performance alone. That would require a more direct test and preferably a performance-referenced direct test. If, for example we are interested in screening applicants for a course in Management Studies we may be interested in their note-taking ability. We might set up a simulated lecture and specify *in advance* that acceptable candidates should be able to record 80 per cent of the information given during the lecture. If our studies of the criterion performance have indicated that this is the minimum performance acceptable to participate in the course (though this may not be so easy to establish), then even if every prospective candidate fails this test we would have no reason to change the pass-mark. We might want to look at the construction, administration and scoring in order to check that the candidate's performance was a true reflection of his proficiency but if there was nothing wrong here the conclusion would have to be that none of the candidates was suitable for the course. This conclusion would have been impossible if we had used an indirect test because there would have been no way of setting the pass-mark independently of the scores of some particular group of candidates.

The setting of standards in this way is called **criterion-referencing**. Although more satisfying (and, it is often claimed, *fairer*) than norm-referencing, such an approach does have its drawbacks. Firstly, it may be difficult to establish just what the minimum acceptable level of performance is. (Why 80 per cent? why not 90; or 70?). Secondly, the direct test, as we have seen, has its own unique problems of administration and measurement. The discrete-point test is much easier to administer and score even if there are subsequent problems about what the scores actually mean. A trade-off is operating here between convenience and validity.

## 3.5  Summary

It has been established that the psychometric approach to language testing is an indirect system-referenced approach. The linguistic analysis on which it is based nowaways seems incomplete and limited although it should be said that modern practitioners do not seem to adhere rigorously to it.

The discrete-point formats used by this approach bring considerable gains in administrative convenience although care must be taken during test construction to establish exactly which aspects of proficiency are being addressed by any given item. The possibility that the format itself may influence the results as well as the candidate's proficiency has been indicated by recent research.

The indirect nature of these test types makes it difficult to establish the difficulty of a test and thus interpret any given score. This may be done by norm-referencing to the test population providing this is large and stable enough.

The alternative to norm-referencing is to establish standards independently of given scores by inspecting the test and criterion performances. This is termed criterion-referencing and can only be done with a direct kind of test with its associated problems of administration and measurement.

# 4

# The use and interpretation of statistics

## 4.1 The surrogate judgement

This chapter sets out to give an idea of the kinds of statistical techniques which are available to the language tester and to what extent they can contribute to the development and use of tests. We will also be interested in looking at how such techniques may *not* be helpful, in that their use may obscure important issues, sometimes giving a spurious significance to results which, looked at from a more commonsense point of view, may be less impressive. The fact is that the last century has seen the development of statistical methods of considerable sophistication. Their usefulness in the natural and social sciences is unquestionable when the behaviour of large populations is to be investigated. In the field of second-language learning, however, their application is not so straightforward: populations are often quite small, the number of relevant variable factors quite high. In addition, the development of the kind of theoretical models which would guide and justify the employment of such techniques is at an early stage.

For all of these reasons there are limits to the level of sophistication at which language-test data can be statistically treated. In spite of this, the easy availability of statistical 'packages' on university computers has encouraged the wholesale application of all kinds of statistical tools to data which do not always merit such treatment. We will touch on some of these techniques at the end of the chapter but our main concern will be to look at the sort of 'bread and butter' methods which serve as an adjunct to the user's commonsense rather than as a replacement for it.

## 4.2 Questions with statistical answers

Statistical techniques help with the making of judgements and decisions at two stages: first, during the development of tests, and later, when they are being used. If a test is being developed seriously it will go through one or more stages of **piloting** when it is tried out on a suitable group of 'guinea-pigs'. Questions which must be answered at this stage are:

> Did the candidates in general perform well or badly?
> How do they compare with other groups who have taken the same test?
> How do the results on this test compare with the results on other tests which these candidates have taken?
> How much does the test spread the candidates out?
> How closely do the scores on one part of the test correspond to scores on other parts?
> Are any of the sections or items very easy or very difficult?
> Are any of the sections or items behaving strangely?
> How closely do the performances on this test reflect performances on other tests?

The answers to the above questions will enable the writer to modify the test to make it serve its purpose more effectively or economically. When it comes to using the test for decision-making purposes, analyses of the results will allow the user to base decisions on more explicit criteria:

> Is this a 'good' score?
> What should the pass-mark be?
> How much correspondence is there between these results and other measurements of the candidate's ability?
> How much agreement is there between scorers of subjectively marked parts of the test?
> How much confidence should be placed in the results of the test?

Before we go on to consider these points in detail two things should be made clear.

Although the kinds of statistical tool we shall be examining are inevitably associated with the 'psychometric' school of testing outlined in the last chapter, this does not mean that such techniques cannot be used for the development of other kinds of test. Just as the item formats developed by this school can be borrowed without subscribing to the accompanying theory of language, many of the techniques for presenting and analysing results are also relevant to other 'task-based' test types. We shall be looking at such applications in detail in Chapter 6.

The second point has to do with the statistical behaviour of a test and its validity. A satisfactory performance according to all the criteria listed above (with the possible exception of the correlation with other tests) does not guarantee that the content of the test is drawn from the relevant domain. For example, a multiple-choice general knowledge test could be written in English which would meet all the statistical requirements for a good entrance test in that the items performed well and the test scores were well spread out across the score range. It would be quite useless, however, as an entrance test for a French language programme because there is no reason to believe that the candidates' scores reflected their mastery of French. In indirect test types, statistical analysis cannot guarantee that criterion proficiency is properly derived from criterion performance or that it is sampled properly. Item analysis may point to the failure of test performance to reflect test proficiency by showing up 'trick questions'. In general, however, while the difficulty of a test may be assessed statistically, its relevance can only be established empirically or by inspection.

# 4.3 Describing the population

If a group of candidates take a test then there will be a range of scores from the highest to the lowest. An easy way to see how these scores are distributed through the group is to plot a **histogram** in which the height of each column is proportional to the number of candidates falling into the corresponding score band. If we are testing something like intelligence and the sample is large enough, the histogram will have a 'bell-shaped' profile with most of the candidates scoring in the middle and fewer at the upper and lower ends of the range.

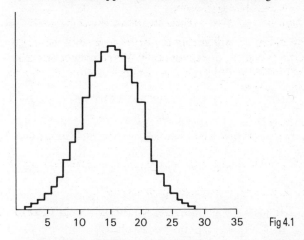

Fig 4.1

This kind of shape is produced by tests of characteristics which are 'normally distributed' throughout the population; that is, the population contains a random selection of individuals without any special bias in their selection.

Language tests do not always produce this sort of result because they are often taken by groups that are far from random samples as far as language proficiency is concerned; they may consist of candidates who have been prepared for the test or have been selected as a special group for teaching purposes. For this reason the neat bell-shaped curve of the normal distribution is not often seen in language-test histograms. Figure 4.2 is more typical.

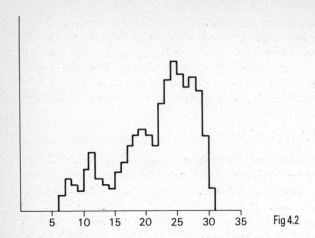

Fig 4.2

## 4.3.1 Quantifying the distribution: means and variance

The first piece of information which can be obtained by examining the histogram is how difficult the candidates in general found the test. If the bulk of the candidates lie in the upper half of the score bands then the test was quite easy for most of them (e.g. in Figure 4.3 above). If the 'hump' is in the lower half the test was difficult for most candidates. This general observation can be expressed more precisely by calculating the **mean** of the results. This is done by adding all the results together and dividing by the number of candidates. The result (21 in the case of Figure 4.2 – over half marks) gives some kind of idea of the general performance of the group.

There is another aspect which is important though: consider these two sets of results:

| | |
|----|----|
| 43 | 24 |
| 51 | 70 |
| 57 | 7 |
| 42 | 92 |
| 56 | 26 |
| 48 | 78 |

Both have the same mean (49.5). But clearly the results are distributed very differently in the two groups. The second set shows much more difference between scores than the first, where they are 'bunched' together. The second group is said to show greater **variance** than the first. This is another dimension of distribution which can be important for certain applications. It too, can be expressed numerically. This is done by measuring the difference between each score and the mean. These are called the **deviations**. The larger these deviations then the more the test is 'spreading out' the candidates across the score range. Calculating an average value for the deviations is not so straightforward, though. If we simply added them up and took the mean, the result would be zero because some of the values are negative and would exactly cancel out the positive deviations.

In order to get round this, the deviations are squared so that all values are positive. Then a mean is taken and the value obtained is called the **variance** of the results.

By taking the square root of this figure the **standard deviation** is obtained. We can regard this as the amount that the average result lies away from the mean. The greater it is, the more spread out the results and vice-versa. (The standard deviations for the two sets of scores above are 5.8 and 31.7 respectively.)

Why should we be interested in this value? To answer this question we have to look at what these measures of distribution actually mean to the test writer or user.

## 4.3.2 Interpreting the statistics

The histogram and the two numerical values give information about the distribution of scores among the candidates who have taken a test. The values are the result of an interaction between the candidates and the test. On the basis of the analysis we can draw conclusions, either about the test or the group of candidates – but not both. It would be quite unreasonable to expect information both about an unknown population and an untried test on the basis of such an analysis. An example should make this clear:

If the mean score of a group of candidates on a test was 23 per cent then we can safely say that the candidates found the test difficult. If we know the test well and have used it with comparable candidates in the past who usually score around 50–60 per cent then we can say that this group seems to be particularly poor. If, on the other hand, the test is a new one and is being tried out on a group of candidates which we know and who will eventually take it for decision-making purposes, then we can see that the test is very difficult. Unless there are reasons why we want to keep it difficult, we may decide that it is *too* difficult and will have to be made easier. We cannot, however, decide *both* that the test was difficult *and* the candidates poor in the absence of evidence from sources other than this one administration. The statistical analysis will give information about the population if the behaviour of the test is known, or about the test if the behaviour of the population is known – but not both.

Similar considerations apply to the interpretation of the standard deviation. Since this is a measure of how much the scores are spread out on each side of the mean, it is of particular interest in developing tests whose purpose is to spread candidates out as much as possible (e.g. placement tests). A high standard deviation may be an indication that the test is discriminating strongly between candidates. It may also be an indication that there is an extremely wide range of proficiency levels among the candidates. If we know nothing about the population or the test it is impossible to choose between these two interpretations. If, on the other hand, we know something about the population then the standard deviation will tell us something about the test. A test administered to the entire population of a language school from beginners to advanced students would be expected to produce results with a high standard deviation because of the wide range of proficiency levels in the population. Failure to give this expected high value would be evidence that the test was failing to reflect the range of levels in the population and would call into question the adequacy of the test as, say, a placement test. Conversely if a test's discriminatory powers have already been established then a group of candidates whose results have a low standard deviation can be safely regarded as being fairly homogeneous – the 'bunching' of the scores truly reflects a narrow proficiency range rather than being an artifact of a test which does not discriminate very much. Again, the analysis will only give information about the distribution of proficiency in the population if its behaviour with other, known populations has been established.

### 4.3.3 Using distribution statistics to make decisions about tests

We have discussed a little what these statistics mean. Now we have to consider ways in which they can be used. One of their most important functions is to help decision-making during the trial or **piloting** of a test. This usually involves administering the test to a known population so that the analysis will throw light on the behaviour of the test. The following questions can be answered by a statistical analysis:

An examination of the mean will show how difficult or easy the test was (relative to the abilities of the test population). If the population is known and we are clear about the test and its future purposes then the mean allows us to check if the test as a whole is too difficult or too easy.

If the test consists of several parts (sometimes called **sub-tests**), a comparison of the means of the sub-tests may show that candidates tended to score higher on some parts than on others. This may be unwelcome news if the scores on the separate sub-tests are going to be totalled to provide an overall score. If such an analysis reveals, say, that the reading sub-test produced a mean score which was half the size of the other sub-tests; then when the total is made the reading sub-test will contribute only about half as much to the total score as the other tests. If our analysis of the criterion performance leads us to consider reading skills to have equal importance, then something must be done to redress the balance. In this case, doubling the reading scores before adding them to the total will do the trick. In general, we can make sure the contribution of the sub-test scores to the total is balanced by **weighting** the scores of each sub-test by a factor derived from a comparison of the means.

### 4.3.4 Using distribution statistics – three case studies

To give a clearer idea of how the above statistical methods can be used it may be helpful to look at three practical applications.

#### Case 1 – choosing a placement test
Let us imagine that a language school is dissatisfied with its current placement test (perhaps too many misplacements are occurring) and wishes to replace it with a new one. Three possible tests have been obtained from various sources and one must be chosen. The tests are administered to a representative sample of students (at least fifty) drawn from across the range of classes. For each test the mean and standard deviation are calculated and a histogram plotted. The results are as follows:

|        | mean | s.d. |
|--------|------|------|
| Test 1 | 27.1 | 14.5 |
| Test 2 | 29.2 | 13.4 |
| Test 3 | 24.3 | 13.7 |

Since the function of a placement test is to discriminate strongly between candidates in order to place them as accurately as possible, one of the characteristics of a good placement test is a high standard deviation. A quick glance at the figures shows that Test 1 has the highest s.d. Does this make it the most suitable test? Not necessarily. If we examine the tests more closely we will see that the maximum possible mark for Tests 1 and 2 is 60, whereas Test 3 is out of 50. In order to compare the deviations correctly we must express them as a proportion of the total mark. Dividing the deviations by the totals we get:

| Test 1 | $14.5/60 = 0.241$ |
|--------|-------------------|
| Test 2 | $13.4/60 = 0.227$ |
| Test 3 | $13.7/60 = 0.274$ |

This value (sometimes known as the coefficient of discrimination) reveals that Test 3 is spreading out the candidates more effectively than the other two tests. All things being equal, then, we should prefer Test 3 over the other two tests.

An important point needs to be made here. The statistical behaviour of a test is only one of a number of factors which need to be taken into account when assessing its suitability. Satisfactory statistical parameters do not in themselves guarantee that the content of the test will match the pedagogic philosophy of the teaching situation. Only inspection will reveal this. Also, considerations about ease of administration and marking may have as much or more weight than statistical aspects. The important point is that a statistical analysis only provides one of a number of considerations which bear upon the selection of the test.

## Case 2 – Moderating end-of-course assessment

As a second example let us consider a course being followed by a number of parallel classes. At the end of the course students can pass on to the next level if their achievement of the course objectives has been satisfactory both as measured by a terminal test and also according to a grade assigned by the class teacher along the following lines:

A – has more than achieved the course objectives
B – has comfortably achieved the course objectives
C – has only just achieved the course objectives
D – has not achieved the course objectives

The exam is used to check that teachers are assigning grades according to a roughly similar policy, and also as a basis for negotiation if discrepancies should arise.

The exam is administered to the classes and at the same time letter grades are assigned by the class teachers. When the exam has been marked the results are grouped together by letter grade and the mean and standard deviation calculated for each group.

Typical results might be as follows:

| | | |
|---|---|---|
| A students | mean 115 | s.d. 8.61 |
| B students | mean 101 | s.d. 10.0 |
| C students | mean 86 | s.d. 6.64 |
| D students | mean 69 | s.d. 7.31 |

Next a graph is plotted with the scores along the horizontal axis, and for each group a line is drawn with the mean at its centre and one standard deviation on each side of it. Each line then represents the typical range of scores for students in the group.

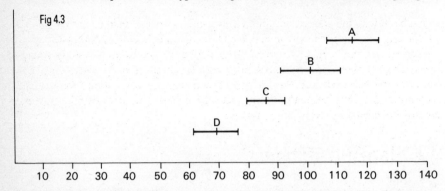

Fig 4.3

There is some overlap, of course as the correspondence between exam result and letter grade is unlikely to be perfect. Individual scores can be checked off against letter grade. A few discrepancies are to be expected, but if the students in one class have scores which are consistently outside the score ranges for their letter grades, this indicates that the grading policy of the teacher concerned is out of line with that of the others and some negotiation may be needed.

## Case 3 – Weighting sub-tests

A test may consist of a number of sub-tests with the same total score for each since the test proficiencies which are probed by each sub-test are considered to have equal importance. Nevertheless, after administration some sub-tests may turn out to be more difficult or easier than expected and the range of scores in each test will differ markedly. When the scores are added together to make a total, the low scores of the difficult sub-tests will contribute less to this total than the easier tests. This is undesirable if they are considered to have equal weight. These discrepancies can be evened out by using a factor derived from a consideration of the means of the sub-tests.

For example, a test may consist of five sub-tests with the following mean scores:

| | |
|---|---|
| Subtest A | 15.7 |
| Subtest B | 10.2 |
| Subtest C | 6.7 |
| Subtest D | 16.4 |
| Subtest E | 9.2 |
| Total | 58.2 |

If all the subtests had contributed equally to the total each would have had a mean of:

$$58.2/5 = 11.64$$

To make the mean of sub-test A equal to 11.64 we must multiply by:

$$11.64/15.7 = 00.74$$

The factors for the other sub-tests are:

| | |
|---|---|
| Subtest B | 1.14 |
| Subtest C | 1.73 |
| Subtest D | 0.71 |
| Subtest E | 1.27 |

Each student sub-score is multiplied by the appropriate factor for that sub-test. In this way each sub-test will be making an equal contribution to the total.

Again it is important to stress that the statistical technique is merely a way of presenting the scores in a more balanced way. It is not a remedy where imbalances between the sub-tests are due to poor test design or administration. Statistical techniques can only refine the use of measures whose adequacy or relevance have already been established by other means.

# 4.4 Ranking statistics

The statistics we have been looking at so far concern the scores of candidates as an absolute measure of their performance on the test. It is also possible to represent a candidate's result in terms of his position relative to other candidates who have taken the same test.

## 4.4.1 The rank score

The simplest example of such a measure is the **rank score**. This is simply the position of the candidate in the ranked order of the group: 1st, 2nd, 21st, etc. This is a familiar way of presenting exam results in secondary school classes. Clearly the rank score does not give us as much information as the original (or **raw**) score since we need to know about the overall composition of the test group in order to decide what it means. It can be useful, however, in monitoring the performance of a learner across a series of progress tests. If the rank score of a student suddenly drops from around third to fifteenth then the teacher may need to investigate further.

## 4.4.2 Percentile scores

A more sophisticated version of the rank score is obtained by calculating for each candidate the percentage of the test population which scored less than him. Thus the bottom candidate in the group will have a percentile score of 0, and that of the top candidate will be nearly 100. Again the information which such scores provide will depend on our knowledge of the test population. These scores are often used for assigning grades and passes to examination candidates. The procedure is as follows.

Firstly, two axes are drawn with 100 divisions vertically, and horizontally as many divisions as there are marks in the exam. Starting with the bottom candidate and working up, for each candidate the percentage of lower-scoring candidates is calculated and plotted against the actual score on the horizontal axis. This typically gives a vaguely sigmoid curve known as a **cumulative distribution polygon:**

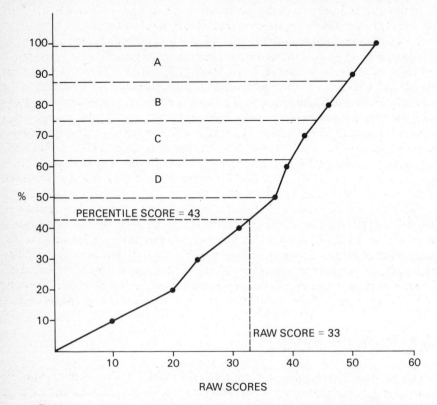

Fig 4.4

This can then be used to convert any candidate's raw score into a percentile score by drawing a line from the raw score on the horizontal axis to the curve. The vertical position of the intercept with the curve gives the percentile score. For example, in the case above a raw score of 33 corresponds to a percentile score of 43.

This curve can be used for deciding pass-marks and grades by a technique very common in the American educational system and among public examinations in Britain. A decision is made to pass, say 50 per cent of the candidates. A line is drawn across from the 50th percentile. The pass-mark is obtained by reading off the horizontal axis at the point where the line intersects the curve. In this case the pass-mark is 37.

It may be decided to allow four passing grades, A, B, C, and D. The top 50 percentile scores are divided into bands of 12.5 per cent each. By drawing lines at this interval, the raw scores which delimit the bands can be read off the curve. In this case they are:

| | |
|---|---|
| A | 49+ |
| B | 44 – 48 |
| C | 40 – 43 |
| D | 37 – 39 |

In this way 12.5 per cent of the candidates get an A, 12.5 per cent a B, etc. Fifty per cent fail regardless how proficient they were in absolute terms.

This may seem a rather arbitrary and unfair way of assigning grades, and yet, as we saw earlier (3.4), such norm-referencing can be justified where the degree of difficulty of an exam is difficult to establish by inspection alone and where the population is likely to be more stable from one administration to the other than the difficulty of the test. The alternative, if we are confident of the level of the test, is to assign grades and passes on the basis of the raw scores, saying, for example, that candidates scoring 85 per cent or more will receive an A Grade. If no candidates achieve this level then there will simply be no Grade As assigned at that administration. Great confidence is necessary, however, in the test and its manner of construction in order to choose such a policy. The more indirect the test is then the more difficult this policy becomes to implement.

Often the pass and grade cut-off marks are decided during the piloting of a test, i.e. before it gets used on a 'real' population. The pilot population may be learners from a known range of classes in a language school, thus giving the percentile scores some kind of meaning, but in essence this is little different from the ordinary norm-referencing procedure outlined above. The decision whether to use these techniques ultimately rests on whether the test writer or user believes the behaviour of his test to be more or less stable than that of the population it is administered to.

# 4.5 Item analysis

So far we have been looking at statistical devices which enable us to monitor the behaviour of whole tests or sub-tests in their interaction with populations. Now we have to examine techniques used for probing the performance of individual questions or items. There are several of these available but the two most widely used are the facility index and the discrimination index. These can be calculated for each item in the test and they reveal, respectively, which proportion of the candidates responded correctly to the item and to what extent high-scorers on the test as a whole did better on that item than low-scorers.

## 4.5.1  The facility index

This is calculated by counting how many of the test population responded correctly to the item and dividing by the total number of candidates. Thus, if in a sample of 60 candidates, 43 responded correctly then the item has a facility index of:

$$43/60 = 0.72$$

This index can be useful when deciding the order of items in a sub-test. It is generally desirable to start the test with an easy item. During piloting, such items can be identified and the one with the highest facility index put in first position. In a placement test, if saving time is important and we do not want candidates struggling with items which they have no chance of answering correctly, the items in the test can be put in order of increasing difficulty. Candidates can then be instructed to stop when they start meeting items which they cannot answer.

## 4.5.2  The discrimination index

The discrimination index is a classical piece of psychometric testing apparatus and, as such, embodies the guiding principle of the approach with all its strengths and drawbacks. Before we look at these in detail let us briefly examine how it is calculated.

If a group of candidates answers an item, some of them will respond correctly and some incorrectly. By organizing the candidates according to their scores on the whole test we can divide them into three groups: the high-scorers, the middle-scorers and the low scorers. There are various ways of drawing the lines but for technical reasons the bottom and top 27 per cent are taken as low and high scorers respectively. For each item we can then count how many answered correctly in each group. If more high scorers than low scorers answered correctly then the item is distinguishing between strong and weak candidates and is said to be a good discriminator. If the numbers are the same or (heaven forbid!) more low scorers responded correctly, then the item is suspect and may need to be changed.

The calculation is as follows:

$$\text{Index of discrimination} = \frac{t - b}{N}$$

Where   t = no. of correct responses in the top group
b = no. of correct responses in the bottom group
N = no. of candidates in one of the groups

It can have the value from $+1.0$ (all high-scorers responded correctly and no low scorers) through $0.0$ (the numbers are equal), to $-1.0$ (all the low scorers responded correctly and no high-scorers – a very anomalous result).

To take an example: if 60 candidates take a test, after arranging them in rank order we take the top and bottom 27 per cent which works out at 16 in each group. We count the number of correct responses in each group:

Top group          9
Bottom group       4

$$\text{Index} = \frac{9 - 4}{16} = 0.31$$

The item is a moderate discriminator.

If the number of correct responses in the lower group exceeds that in the upper group then we get a negative index. This may happen if the item contains some 'trap' which more advanced learners fall into while the weaker ones, in blissful ignorance, avoid:

Can you tell me  (a)  where do you live?
                (b)  where you live?
                (c)  where live you?
                (d)  where you do live?

The above item sometimes produces negative indices with elementary learners since the stronger students recognize the question form (a) as being familiar, while the weaker students, having no idea about English question forms, tend to go for (b) which looks more straightforward and in this case happens to be correct. With more advanced learners the problem would not arise and the item would probably behave normally. This illustrates the point that item-analysis data, like other statistical measures, have no absolute value but vary from one kind of population to another.

## 4.5.3  Distractor analysis

The item analysis techniques examined above work on the basis of whether candidates responded correctly or incorrectly. In the case of a multiple-choice test we can go further and examine the distribution of responses between the correct answer and the incorrect alternatives (known as **distractors**). Various kinds of analysis are possible. We can simply count how many chose each alternative:

Sasha comes from Tunisia, (a)  comes he?           0
                     (b)  isn't he?            37
                     (c)  doesn't he?      13
                     (d)  is he?            10

In this case we can see that no candidates were tempted to choose (a) and we might decide to change the distractor to something more attractive.

Alternatively we could measure the mean total scores on the sub-test of all the candidates who chose each distractor:

The bar is (a) in the top floor.          56%
           (b)  on                    71%
           (c)  at                     61%
           (d)  to                    46%

In this case we can see that those who chose the correct response did better in the test overall than those who chose the distractors. If this had not been the case then the item would have had to be looked at since its discrimination would not have been satisfactory. It should be mentioned that this kind of analysis is extremely tedious and time-consuming to do by hand and, in the absence of suitably lobotomized assistants, is better done by computer.

## 4.5.4  Why do item analysis?

One of the immediate benefits of item analysis is, as we have seen, to draw the attention of the test designer to items which contain problems or ambiguities in their construction which escaped notice during the construction of the test. As such, it is a useful adjunct to the test developer's own judgement and experience. However, there are aspects of the technique which, being related to its origins in classical psychometric testing, make its uncritical use a little problematic for the language tester.

The goal of psychometric test development is to produce a test which will discriminate as strongly as possible along the parameter which has been chosen as the target of the test. Item analysis permits the identification of items which are too difficult or too easy (outside the range 0.25 to 0.75 facility value is sometimes quoted) or which fail to discriminate strongly enough between candidates (index of discrimination lower than about 0.3). After item analysis the test can be tinkered with to remove or rewrite unsatisfactory items and thus maximize the discriminating power of the test as a whole. This is possible since, as we have seen in the last chapter, the items are 'discrete', i.e. the presence of one question does not affect the candidate's performance on the others. The items can be considered to behave quite independently of each other.

Two points need to be made here. The first concerns the irrelevance of test content to this kind of test development. The criterion for the inclusion or exclusion of items is entirely statistical. An item which is 'too easy' according to psychometric criteria should be eliminated because it will probably fail to discriminate. The non-psychometric test writer might protest at this point that, easy though it may be, the item should be retained since it tests an aspect of proficiency about which he needs information. Even if every candidate answers it correctly this is entirely acceptable since it indicates that every candidate has mastered the proficiency feature which the item is probing. The objection reveals a fundamental distinction between psychometric and non-psychometric approaches concerning the dimensionality of the constructs being used. This leads on to the second point.

## 4.5.5  Measures, scales and lists

When we measure an aspect of ability there are a number of different forms that the measure can take. Crudely speaking there are three possibilities: a scale, a number of scales, or a list. Taking a non-linguistic example: to measure the acuity of someone's hearing, one scale is sufficient and different individuals could be positioned at different points along this scale according to the value of the smallest sound they could detect. The data are unidimensional.

In order to measure physical strength, on the other hand, we would need several scales, one for each muscle group. We could place individuals along a single scale by simply adding their various strengths together but this would obscure important differences and not do justice to the data which are multidimensional.

If, however, we wanted to measure how well-read a person was, the most appropriate measure would be a list of the most important books he had read in various fields. A straight count of the number of books would be unsatisfactory since it is the range and quality of texts read which determines erudition and not mere quantity. In this case the most appropriate measure would be a list.

When it comes to language ability, which is the most appropriate kind of measure to use? Well, for teaching purposes we can see that use is made of all of them to some degree, although there seems to be a preference for lists. Structurally and functionally based courses tend to make use of lists of language features when specifying course content. On the other hand, receptive skills such as listening are often thought of as simple 'strengths' which can be measured on a one-dimensional scale.

A variety of reading skills may be distinguished (skimming, scanning, intensive, etc.) necessitating several scales for their measurement.

Now we are in a position to see why the techniques of psychometric testing may be at odds with the goals of language pedagogy. As we saw in the last chapter (3.2.2.) psychometric testers traditionally divided language proficiency into a number of compartments, each one of which could be probed with a sub-test. Now, and this is the important point, the feature which is measured by each sub-test was assumed to be unidimensional and the results were capable of being represented as positions on a single scale. The weeding out of low-discriminating items is done on the grounds that high-scoring candidates on the test as a whole should do better on every item than low-scorers. In this way each item is 'pushing in the same direction', pushing the high-scorers towards the top of the scale and the low-scorers towards the bottom to give maximal separation or discrimination. Items which do not contribute to this process are eliminated by the item analysis.

Now we can see how conflict can arise. Let us take a multiple-choice grammar test. If an item testing, say, 'knowledge of *some* and *any* as quantifiers' is successfully answered by almost all the candidates the psychometrist will want to remove it because it does not contribute to the overall discrimination of the test. He may wish to replace it with an item testing, say, knowledge of verb tenses. Since he conceives of knowledge of grammar as a unidimensional 'strength', he will be untroubled by the change of domain from which the item is sampling. But, the language teacher objects, what about knowledge of quantifiers? I need information about this area. Since he regards knowledge of grammar as a list of repertoire from which he wishes to sample rather than a simple unidimensional strength, the statistical behaviour of an item is less important to him than that it should sample from the correct domain.

This then is the core of the problem about using psychometric techniques for language-test development. The test writer must decide to what extent he wishes to subscribe to the unidimensional assumption of the psychometrist and to what extent the domain from which test content is drawn has more importance. As mentioned earlier, receptive skills, especially listening, lend themselves more readily to one-dimensional treatment. It is possible, however, to distinguish different types of listening and in a fully-fledged performance-referenced test we might wish to characterize listening ability in terms of a repertoire of concrete tasks which the candidate must perform. In this case we would give little weight to psychometric considerations in test development since the various parts of the test would be retained on the basis of their relevance to some future goal rather than the distribution of their results. The important thing is that whatever choice is made, the implications of the decision be borne in mind. Psychometric statistical techniques provide a useful set of tools for monitoring and refining test development, but it is important to be sure that we really wish to subscribe to the underlying principles of the school before whole-heartedly embracing its methods.

# 4.6 The relation between measures – the correlation coefficient

If a group of candidates takes two tests then there may be more or less correspondence between the scores. If candidates who score highly on one test tend to score highly on the other and *vice versa*, the two sets of scores are said to be correlated. If, on the other hand, no such relationship can be discerned then they are uncorrelated. The degree of relationship can be quantified and expressed as the correlation coefficient. The most widely used way of doing this is called the Pearson Product Moment Coefficient calculated according to the following formula:

$$r = \Sigma \frac{D_a D_b}{N s_a s_b}$$

Where $r$ = the product moment coefficient
$\quad D_a$ = the deviation of a score in test a
$\quad D_b$ = the deviation of a score in test b
$\quad D_a D_b$ = the sum of the products of the deviations
$\quad N$ = the number of candidates
$\quad s_a$ = the standard deviation of the scores on test a
$\quad s_b$ = the standard deviation of the scores on test b

The correlation coefficient is calculated in such a way that its value may range from $+1.0$ (perfect correlation) through 0 (no correlation), to $-1.0$ (perfect inverse correlation, i.e. high scorers on one test are low scorers on the other).

A typical correlation coefficient between different kinds of language test would be 0.6 Where the tests are very similar, correlation coefficients as high as 0.9 or more may be recorded. Where the tests are dissimilar (listening tests and grammar tests for example), correlation coefficients of 0.4 or 0.5 are to be expected.

## 4.6.1 The scattergram

Another way of showing the degree of relationship between two sets of results is to plot a **scattergram**. This is done by plotting a point for each candidate on a two-dimensional grid such that the vertical position of the point represents the score on one test and the horizontal position the score on the other. If the tests are highly correlated the points will form a cigar-shaped cloud lying along the diagonal of the grid:

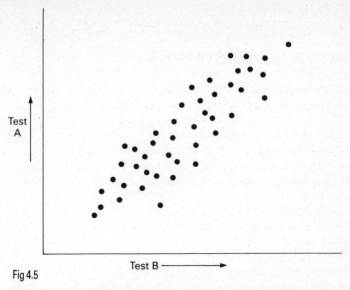

Fig 4.5

Uncorrelated tests produce a random sprinkling of points. While the scattergram can give a good visual impression of the degree of correlation of two sets of scores, it is obviously more difficult to compare different correlations and the correlation coefficient is more appropriate for the latter purpose.

## 4.6.2 The correlation matrix

When a number of tests are administered to the same population each will have a correlation with each of the others. These inter-correlations can be shown on a correlation matrix:

|  | 1 | 2 | 3 | 4 | 5 |
|---|---|---|---|---|---|
| 1 Error detection | * | 694 | 603 | 586 | 524 |
| 2 Grammar | 694 | * | 671 | 670 | 556 |
| 3 Reading | 603 | 671 | * | 540 | 425 |
| 4 Vocabulary | 586 | 670 | 540 | * | 462 |
| 5 Writing | 524 | 556 | 425 | 462 | * |

Fig 4.6

The diagonal positions are left blank since they represent the correlation of a test with itself. Using this particular method of calculation the coefficients would be, rather uninformatively, 1.0.

## 4.6.3 The use and interpretation of correlation coefficients

As we have seen, the correlation coefficient is a way of expressing the degree of relationship between two sets of results. Used carefully, this technique can be used to solve two recurrent problems in language testing.

The first problem is that of finding a quick and easy test to do the job of an elaborate and time-consuming one. (See 2.2.2. for an example of this.) By administering both tests to the same population we can examine the correlation between the scores to see if this is high enough for one to be used as a substitute for the other. (But see below for *caveats* concerning this practice.)

The second problem which correlation coefficients can help to solve is the much knottier one of deciding what exactly a test is testing and if different tests are measuring 'the same thing' or not. The use of correlation coefficients is based on the same psychometric presupposition examined earlier, i.e. that each sub-test is a measure of a single unidimensional 'strength'. If the correlation coefficient between two sets of scores is sufficiently high, we may, in certain circumstances, conclude that roughly the same dimension of proficiency is being measured by each test. If, on the other hand, the correlation coefficient is low, we can (again under certain circumstances) conclude that the two aspects of proficiency which the test is measuring are relatively distinct. The use of these sorts of statistics and the related techniques of factorial analysis in order to explore the structure of language proficiency has generated considerable controversy in the last few years. These arguments will be examined in greater detail in the next chapter.

One practical use of this idea is to eliminate sub-tests from a battery of tests for reasons of economy. If there is a high correlation between the scores on two sub-tests then one of them may be eliminated on the grounds that it is 'doing the same job' as the other. As with item analysis, considerations of content may outweigh the statistical arguments. If we are interested in having information about the domain of each test then both must be retained although from a strictly psychometric point of view they represent an unnecessary duplication of effort. A decision about this will obviously depend on the purpose of the test battery.

## 4.6.4 Handle with care

As a means of distorting and misrepresenting data, the correlation coefficient is possibly one of the most pernicious statistical devices ever invented. Certain aspects of its behaviour make it necessary to examine very carefully all claims based on the use of this index.

Firstly, the size of the correlation coefficient is notoriously dependent on the range of scores in each test and it is particularly sensitive to the presence of 'extreme cases', i.e. candidates who score very high or low on both tests.

Take the following scores, which have a correlation coefficient of 0.434:

Test A: 12, 8, 14, 9, 13, 14, 15, 7, 9, 17
Test B: 10, 12, 11, 7, 10, 12, 14, 10, 14, 14

The addition of a very good candidate who scores 18 and 19 pushes the correlation coefficient up to 0.625 and the addition of a near-zero candidate (1, 2) pushes it up even further to 0.802. This property of the measure facilitates all kinds of illegitimate techniques such as deliberately introducing extreme cases into the sample in order to boost the correlation coefficients to a level where they support the desired thesis.

For this reason a correlation coefficient reported alone is not very informative because we do not know the composition of the population which generated it. Only when correlation coefficients are presented for comparison with correlation coefficients between other tests administered to the same population can reliable conclusions be based upon them.

The second tendency which has to be resisted is the temptation to assume that because the results of two measures are correlated then there is a relationship of causation or identity between the things being measured. An often quoted example of the absurdity that this can lead to is that of the correlation between height and mathematical ability among schoolchildren in industrialized countries. This correlation is quite high because, as children grow, they receive instruction in mathematics. It would be absurd to claim, however, that physical growth 'causes' improved maths ability (or *vice versa*) or that there was a 'common underlying factor' which explained the correspondence. The result is an artefact caused by special treatment of the test population. It would be possible to find other groups of children in the world for whom the correlation would be near zero.

Populations of language testees may also be the recipients of 'special treatment' which often makes the interpretation of correlation coefficients difficult. If a group of learners is taught English composition through an English-medium class, we would expect the listening ability of the group to improve together with their composition skills by dint of listening to the teacher. If we took a group of such learners who had received instruction for different periods of time then we would expect the advanced writers to be better listeners as well. Writing and listening tests administered to this group would show quite high correlations but we would not wish to attribute this to a 'common factor' underlying listening and writing ability. This difficulty with the unambiguous interpretation of correlation coefficients means that extreme caution must be exercised when drawing conclusions from them.

We are on safer ground when we use a low correlation coefficient to exclude the possibility that two tests are measuring the same thing. The following example illustrates this:

A battery of tests contains a multiple-choice sub-test called 'error-detection' in which candidates have to decide which part of a sentence contains an error. This test is claimed to predict proficiency at writing discursive prose. To test this claim the tests are administered to a population together with a writing task similar to the criterion performance for 'writing discursive prose'. (This task is scored according to a band descriptor system of the kind outlined in Chapter 6.) The correlation matrix is prepared:

|                  | 1   | 2   | 3   | 4   | 5   |
|------------------|-----|-----|-----|-----|-----|
| 1 Error detection | *   | 694 | 603 | 586 | 524 |
| 2 Grammar        | 694 | *   | 671 | 670 | 556 |
| 3 Reading        | 603 | 671 | *   | 540 | 425 |
| 4 Vocabulary     | 586 | 670 | 540 | *   | 462 |
| 5 Writing        | 524 | 556 | 425 | 462 | *   |

Fig 4.7

We can see that the correlation coefficient between the writing and the error-detection test is quite low at 0.524. As a predictor of writing performance the grammar test is more effective with a correlation coefficient of 0.556. On the basis of these results we may decide to change or eliminate the error-detection sub-test. It should be emphasized that the use of a low correlation coefficient to exclude the possibility of a relationship between two measures presupposes the reliability of each measure. If one or both of them are unreliable, i.e. the test performance fails to reflect faithfully the test proficiency, or the measurement of the test performance is inconsistent, then no conclusion can be drawn from the results, not even a negative one. In our example we would want to be sure that the learners had the opportunity to perform the writing task to the best of their ability, that no copying occurred and, most importantly, that the different scorers were consistent in their assessment of the resultant texts. Failure to achieve one or more of these conditions would render the writing task useless as a yardstick for assessing the error-detection sub-test.

It should be clear by now that correlation coefficients are very slippery customers indeed and considerable care is needed in their interpretation. We can summarize the *caveats* made above:

1 A correlation coefficient reported in isolation means nothing. It can only be interpreted in comparison with other correlation coefficients between tests administered to the same or comparable populations.
2 A high correlation coefficient between two variables does not entitle us to posit a relationship of causation or identity between them.
3 No conclusion can be drawn about the relationship between two measures on the basis of a correlation coefficient unless both of the measures are reliable, i.e. test performance reflects test proficiency and is consistently assessed.

# 4.7  Calculating reliability

As we saw in 2.2.2 (d), several things may prevent the result of the test from reflecting accurately the candidate's test proficiency. Between the time that the candidate enters the exam room and the result is recorded on the scoresheet, factors may have intervened to subvert the accurate assessment of proficiency. This kind of 'instability' in the measure is termed unreliability. It may result from things outside the test-writer's control: ill-health or excessive nervousness of the candidate. It may derive from the conditions of administration: poor instructions, distractions, cheating, insufficient time. In the case of 'subjectively' scored tests such as composition and oral interview, the biggest barrier to reliable assessment is the inconsistency of the scorer. There are ways of minimizing this (see Chapter 6) and there are ways of calculating how big a problem it is.

## 4.7.1  Inter-rater reliability

Where a numerical mark is assigned to a candidate's performance by an assessor, a check can be made on the reliability by having each performance assessed independently by two assessors. By treating the two scores as results of two tests, the correlation coefficient can be calculated between the two sets of scores. Any value less than 0.7 would be an indication of room for improvement in the briefing of assessors or the system of scoring used.

## 4.7.2 'Hypothetical' reliability

It is unlikely that a group of candidates would take the same test twice within a short period, but if they did then we would expect the results to be more or less the same on each administration (allowing for a small 'practice effect'). This is because the test proficiency which underlies the performance is assumed not to have changed from one administration to the next. Any differences between scores are due therefore to factors other than the test proficiency. Serious discrepancies between the results of the two administrations will therefore call the reliability of the test into question. Reliability measured by re-administering a test and then calculating the correlation coefficient between the two sets of results is called 'test-retest' reliability.

An alternative to re-testing is to compare scores with scores on an equivalent or 'parallel' test. In practice, however, the construction of a suitably equivalent test is a very difficult task. For this reason a similar result can be obtained by splitting the test in half and by treating odd-numbered items as one half and even-numbered items as the other. The correlation between candidates' scores on each half is the 'split-half' reliability estimate.

A computationally equivalent method to the split-half estimate is the Kuder Richardson Formula 20 which can be calculated as follows:

$$K = \frac{n \ (V - \Sigma x.y)}{(n-1) \ V}$$

Where  K = the reliability estimate
       n = number of items in the test
       V = the variance of the test results (see 4.3.1)
       x = the proportion of correct responses to the item.
       y = the proportion of incorrect responses
and Σ x.y = the sum of the products of x and y for each item.

We seem to have come a long way from the use of the test-retest technique. In fact the last two techniques should be regarded more as measures of internal consistency than of reliability.

# 4.8 Factorial analysis

Factorial analysis is a generic name for a group of statistical methods which have been the focus of violent controversy in field of language testing in recent years. The legitimacy of some of the techniques is disputed even by statisticians and often the applicability of these treatments to language test data has not been clearly established. A detailed rehearsal of these disputes would be out of place here but it is worth looking at what the techniques consist of and what promises and pitfalls they hold for the language tester.

## 4.8.1  Looking for patterns in the data

The function of factorial analysis is, broadly speaking, to simplify a variety of sets of scores (which we will call variables) for a given population. This is done by postulating a small number of underlying 'factors', which, by interacting with each other, will give rise to the results which are actually observed. In this way a simple model can account for a complex set of data.

We may take a simple non-linguistic example of how this can be done. We could measure the performance of a group of athletes across a variety of track and field events and record the results for each event. In this case each event would correspond to a 'test'.

1 Long jump
2 Javelin
3 Pole vault
4 High jump
5 Discus
6 100 metre sprint
7 1000 metre run
8 1000 metre swim

Before looking at the actual results we might hypothesize that the performance of an athlete on any particular event is due to the interaction of several factors. One of these will be peculiar to that event (e.g. in the Pole vault the special technique required). The others, however, will be shared with other events (e.g. in the Pole vault 'arm strength' may be a factor which is shared with Swimming, Javelin, etc.). Several of these 'common factors' can be postulated and for the example above we could choose three: 'arm-strength', 'leg-strength' and 'heart-lung efficiency'.

The relevance of each factor to each event can be shown thus:

|                    | arms | legs | heart-lungs |
|--------------------|:----:|:----:|:-----------:|
| 1 Long jump        |      |  +   |             |
| 2 Javelin          |  +   |      |             |
| 3 Pole vault       |  +   |      |             |
| 4 High jump        |      |  +   |             |
| 5 Discus           |  +   |      |             |
| 6 100 metre sprint |      |  +   |             |
| 7 1000 metre run   |      |  +   |      +      |
| 8 1000 metre swim  |  +   |      |      +      |

So far the procedure has been entirely hypothetical. When the results are in, we can see if the actual data confirm the existence of the factors which have been hypothesized. The techniques of factorial analysis can be used to indicate not only that a factor can be discerned and is relevant, but also *how much* the factor contributes to each of the variables. Thus we may find that the leg factor contributes a great deal to the High-jump scores but less to the 1000 metres. This is expressed by saying that the **loading** of the High jump on the leg factor is higher than the loading of the 1000 metres on that factor. How are these loadings calculated?

### 4.8.2 Principal Factor Analysis

Principal Factor Analysis (the most widely-used technique), starts with the assumption that the correlation between two sets of scores is due to the common factors which are shared by the two tests. Thus a high correlation may be expected between Long-jump scores and High-jump scores because of the leg factor which they share. A lower correlation may be expected between Long-jump and Javelin, which have no factors in common. In particular PFA states that the correlation coefficient between two sets of scores is equal to the product of their loadings on the factors which they share. These loadings are worked out in such a way that the hypothetical correlations between tests match as closely as possible the observed correlations. The juggling around of factors and loadings until they match the data is computationally very complex and is normally done by specially-written computer software.

In the case of our example, the factors extracted and the loading of events on them may confirm the existence of the postulated factors. On the other hand a completely different structure may emerge. We might find, for example, only one common factor with high loadings for the first five events and low loadings for the others. Then we would have to hypothesize a 'kinaesthetic control' factor, common to the jumping and throwing events but absent from swimming and running.

This has been an example of 'confirmatory' factorial analysis, in which the technique is used to investigate the existence of previously hypothesized factors. In contrast, 'exploratory' factorial analysis is conducted with no idea what to expect, examining the results to see what turns up. This latter use of the technique is often frowned upon by statisticians and social scientists, since, in the absence of any initially stated hypothesis, it is open to all kinds of imaginative abuse. Unfortunately the use of PFA in analysing data from language tests has a long history of such abuse and, as we shall see in the next chapter, has been almost entirely unhelpful in shedding light on the factors underlying second-language proficiency.

### 4.8.3 Principal Components Analysis

A related technique to PFA is PCA or Principal Components Analysis. A rather simpler technique mathematically, its purpose is to extract factors from the data in such a way that the first factor (now called a Component) which is extracted is as large as possible. It does not work by manipulating the correlation matrix (like PFA) and so therefore certain techniques (such as multiplying factor loadings to get hypothetical correlation coefficients) are not legitimate. Neglect of the distinctions between PCA and PFA has been another source of abuse of these techniques in language testing.

# 4.9 Conclusion – recognizing the limits

It has been the aim of this chapter to induce a certain scepticism about the benefits of statistical analysis to the language tester. While recognizing the usefulness of such techniques in aiding judgement we must also bear in mind that the statistical behaviour of a test or its parts is only one of the factors that determine its relevance or acceptability.

Furthermore, there are limits to what can be revealed by an analysis of statistical data. We must be careful not to go beyond these limits ourselves, and to examine carefully claims made on statistical bases by others.

It may be worth briefly summarizing these limits:

Firstly, the data which are generated by administering a test to a population are a result of the interaction between the test and the population. If the population had been different, different data would have been obtained. In drawing conclusions about the test then we must know something about the population. Failing this, we must limit our conclusions to comparisons between different parts of the test.

Secondly, item-analytical techniques and correlation coefficients as tools for test development assume that each sub-test probes a unidimensional aspect of proficiency. Policies of test development based on these techniques do not always square well with the list-based approaches to describing language proficiency used in many instructional programmes, or with task-based testing techniques. This does not mean that such techniques cannot be used for test development outside the psychometric field but it does mean that the user has to weigh the indications which emerge from them against other considerations of relevance. These can only be established by an examination of the domain from which the test content is drawn and the educational or occupational context within which the test is supposed to work. Indeed, these considerations should precede the choice of statistical techniques to be used during test development. It has been the aim of this chapter to help make that choice an informed one.

# 5

# The integrative
# interlude

## 5.1 The reaction against psychometric testing

When we left the history of language testing in the early 60s, the psychometric approach was firmly established as the dominant orthodoxy in the field. Two aspects of the approach were distinguished: the *instruments* (i.e. discrete-point, closed-response item types) and the *content* (i.e. the hierarchy of skills and levels used to divide up language proficiency for teaching and testing purposes).

During the 60s both the instruments and the analysis of content of this school began to come under critical attack. The first sign of this was a growing interest in what J. B. Carroll, in a much-quoted paper (Carroll, 1961), called *integrative* tests. By this were intended 'holistic' test procedures such as oral interview, composition, dictation. In contrast with 'discrete-point' tests which isolated language features for testing purposes, integrative tests required the testee to demonstrate control of more than one level of language at the same time, sometimes (in the case of dictation) even through two modalities (i.e. listening and writing).

The early arguments in favour of such techniques stressed the unnatural, un-language-like behaviour required of candidates by discrete-point tests, and the desirability of seeing how they could integrate the various components in the performance of more natural-looking tasks. In most cases what was proposed was an adjunct to the discrete-point methods rather than their complete replacement. It should be noted also that the adequacy of the analysis was not questioned, merely the desirability of always testing the components in isolation. Later, however, the analysis itself and the whole set of procedures for the production of language tests came under increasingly severe attack.

The most vociferous of the critics was an American educationalist, John W. Oller (Jr). In a series of articles culminating in the publication of the book *Language Tests at School* (Oller, 1979), he mounted a crusade against what he called 'discrete-point testing'. These publications contained radical proposals concerning the nature and structure of second-language proficiency and the best way to assess it.

What Oller said, in brief, was that language proficiency is indivisible, that tests only differ in their effectiveness at measuring this one factor, and that the elaborate apparatus of dimensions and tests used by the psychometrists could be replaced by *one* test which would directly tap the single indivisible faculty of language proficiency. Tests which were capable of doing this, Oller called 'pragmatic'; they included 'cloze' tests in which the candidate had to restore words blanked out at regular intervals in a text, and dictation, in which the candidate had to write down the words of a text read aloud.

# 5.2  The Unitary Competence hypothesis

Oller called this proposal the 'Unitary Competence hypothesis' (UCH). Rather misleadingly as it happened, since what he meant by 'competence' turns out on examination to have little to do with the notion of competence as it is used by Transformational-Generative grammarians. The term 'proficiency' will therefore be used from now on.

Before going on to examine the nature of this proposed indivisible proficiency let us look at the evidence in its favour.

As we saw in Chapter 3, the psychometric approach was based upon the identification of a number of independent dimensions of language proficiency and the construction of a battery of tests to measure each parameter separately. An important tool in the validation of the tests was the correlation coefficient: a low coefficient between tests purporting to measure different things was evidence (always assuming the tests to be reliable) that they did, in fact, measure different aspects of proficiency. A high correlation between, say, a vocabulary and a grammar test was an indication that one or both of the tests was measuring something from the other's domain. (Though see 4.6.4 for another possible explanation.)

The first indication of something amiss with this neat pigeonholing of tests and language features was the high correlations found between a whole range of discrete-point tests of grammar, vocabulary, etc., and 'integrative' tests like dictation which were much less specific in their targets. Frequently the correlations between discrete-point and integrative tests were higher than between discrete-point tests which were supposed to measure the same thing. This in itself was disturbing since it was difficult to explain in psychometric terms, why the results of two tests measuring, say, vocabulary should have a lower correlation between each other than either of them have with a dictation test which apparently measures a much wider range of elements. Even more embarrassing was the discovery that the highest correlations in the matrix were found between tests like dictations and cloze tests which have in common neither channel (aural as against visual) nor direction (receptive *versus* productive).

These findings undermined the assumption, central to the psychometric approach, that there were distinct dimensions to proficiency and that specific tests could be used to probe them in isolation. Furthermore, the high correlation between laboriously constructed discrete-point tests and tests like cloze and dictation testified, by the very precepts of psychometrics, to the validity of these latter test types which had hitherto been almost universally deprecated.

Oller interpreted these results as an indication of the fundamental inadequacy of the psychometric analysis of language proficiency and the tests used to measure it. The structure which he proposed for this proficiency was quite simple: it had no structure at all. Returning to the diagram used in Chapter 3 to illustrate how psychometric tests are constructed we can see how the criterion proficiency of elements and modalities is derived from 'the Language' and this is then sampled to give a test proficiency which then leads to the test construction:

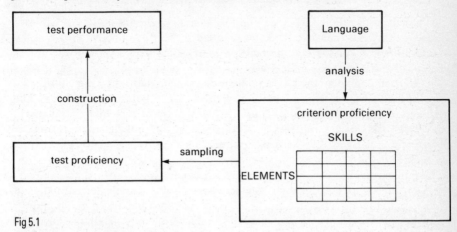

Fig 5.1

Oller's proposal is much simpler:

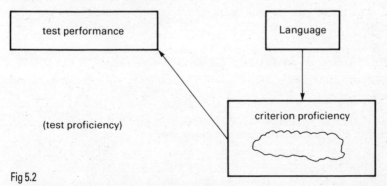

Fig 5.2

The criterion proficiency (i.e. what the user has to know and be able to do in order to use the language) is one amorphous, undifferentiated 'faculty'. There is no point in sampling it since it is indivisible, therefore we skip the test proficiency stage and go straight to the test performance. Any performance (providing it meets certain criteria, detailed below) will, according to Oller, 'tap' the language proficiency of the testee. The metaphor seems to be that of a kind of underground river which can be sampled at any point without appreciable variation in its measured composition (This attractive image permeates much of Oller's writing about language proficiency.)

The existence of this faculty, so the argument goes, explains the statistics: all tests, whatever their label, measure this general factor. Some tests, such as cloze and dictation, measure it better than others. Correlations between such tests are higher than between other tests, such as discrete-point formats, which measure the factor only imperfectly. Differences between tests, then, are a result, not of the different aspects of proficiency which they are measuring, but rather differences in the effectiveness with which they measure one general factor.

## 5.2.1  The evidence from factor-analytic studies

Early evidence for the UCH came from the analysis of the results of test batteries using the factorial analytic techniques outlined in 4.8. It will be recalled that the purpose of these techniques is to simplify a set of data by identifying a small number of factors responsible for differences across a number of variables. The results seemed encouraging for the UCH: in many cases the first factor extracted from the data accounted for a large proportion of the variance between the scores. The loadings of tests like cloze and dictation on this factor were quite high. If this strong first factor did, in fact, represent the unitary language proficiency postulated by Oller then it seemed that these integrative tests were indeed highly effective at measuring it.

The consequences for language testing theory and practice were alarming. The division of language proficiency into levels and skills and the construction of sub-tests to probe each cell of the 'grid' appeared now to be based on an entirely mistaken model of language proficiency. The deliberate focusing on one aspect of proficiency which was part of good psychometric practice, was shown not only to be unfeasible (it had always been difficult to keep sub-tests 'pure' anyway), but also undesirable, since the proper object of language testing now seemed to be a faculty which could not be broken down in this way.

## 5.2.2  The nature of language proficiency – the 'pragmatic expectancy grammar'

So far we have considered only the statistical evidence for the existence of a unitary language factor. As well as proposing a unitary structure for this faculty the UCH also made certain claims about what sort of entity it was.

In order to appreciate Oller's position, it is important to understand that it was a reaction to the principles and practices of psychometric testing. As often happens in these cases, it was in some ways simply the negative image of the orthodoxy which it had rejected.

The first feature of the psychometric approach which Oller challenged was the neglect of context. He noted that the isolation of language elements for testing purposes inevitably resulted in the testee being asked to process samples of decontextualized language; the relationship of the target elements to other parts of the text and to the extralinguistic context had deliberately been made irrelevant to the performance. Extreme examples of this would be the following items:

> ship
> I saw a sheep      (tick the word you hear)
> shop

        making
I've made     a mistake. (tick the correct word)
        make

In the first example, even the surrounding words are no help in identifying the item. To answer the second example correctly the testee must merely be aware of the co-occurrence between the auxiliary and main verbs: not even the meaning of the sentence is pertinent.

Oller pointed out that in normal receptive tasks the context is all-important in identifying ambiguous sounds and words and that the ability to use context to disambiguate in this way was more important than the ability to identify sounds presented in a neutral environment. Doing dictation, for example, required precisely this ability and was therefore a more valid test of the learner's proficiency than isolated recognition tests.

Oller claimed that this ability to process language elements using linguistic and extralinguistic context was identical with the unitary language factor which the statistics appeared to reveal. In reacting against the psychometric account of the structure of language proficiency, Oller made his account everything which the psychometric version was not: where the psychometric proficiency was divisible, Oller's proficiency was unitary; where discrete-point tests eliminated context, in Oller's view, use of context was all; where psychometric tests required esoteric techniques and experts, cloze and dictation tests were simple and straightforward to make and use.

The faculty which was responsible for this context-dependent language processing, Oller called a 'pragmatic expectancy grammar' defining this as 'a psychologically real system which sequentially orders linguistic elements in time and in relation to extra-linguistic context in meaningful ways'. This was the faculty which permitted the production and comprehension of language and was therefore the proper target of language tests. Those tests which 'tapped' this ability (such as cloze and dictation) Oller termed 'pragmatic' tests. Psychometric tests did not meet this 'pragmatic naturalness requirement' and could therefore only imperfectly tap the pragmatic expectancy grammar of the testee.

All of this sounds quite plausible and certainly provided legitimate criticism of some of the excesses of the psychometric approach. Unfortunately Oller's reaction was excessive in the opposite direction. In reinstating the baby which the psychometricians had thrown out with the bath-water, Oller showed himself a little too indulgent towards the returned infant. Serious problems arise when we start to 'unpack' his arguments to see what they might actually mean.

The concept of the 'pragmatic expectancy grammar' unites in a single faculty all the lexical, syntactic, semantic and pragmatic knowledge sources of the user plus the ability to mobilize and integrate them in real-time language activities. In addition to these purely linguistic capacities, the pragmatic expectancy grammar must also include the user's real-world knowledge and the ability to bring it to bear on the performance of a language processing task. However we decide to analyse or describe them, this range of skills is involved in performing any meaningful language task. Now, we may choose not to analyse this mega-faculty; this does not mean to say that it cannot be analysed or that some parts of it may not be differentially developed in different individuals and therefore lead to measurable differences in test performance (even if these differences do not manifest themselves along the neat lines posited by the psychometricians). By choosing to treat what is effectively the entire cognitive-linguistic apparatus of a person as a single, unanalysable entity, we can certainly claim to have put our finger on the faculty responsible for language use, but at the cost of failing to say anything interesting about its structure or development.

At the same time we overlook the very different sorts of processes and representations that are being bundled together under the same name. The term 'pragmatic expectancy grammar' attempts to suggest something rigorous and systematic (a 'grammar'), but at the same time in contact with the real world through 'systematic correspondences' (the 'pragmatic' part). It is never made clear exactly what these correspondence are. Grammars are generally tidy objects while the world (and our knowledge of it) is sprawling and messy and any correspondences between the two orders of representation are unlikely to be systematic in any normal sense of the word. The term 'pragmatic expectancy grammar', then, is difficult to give a coherent meaning to; like 'one-party democracy' it seems to attempt to reconcile two incompatibles using a terminological sleight-of-hand.

The Unitary 'Competence' Hypothesis has implications for language teaching and syllabus design. Since what is to be mastered is 'all of a piece' then the analysis of proficiency into areas of skill or knowledge for teaching purposes is pointless; any meaningful language activity will develop proficiency which will later manifest itself in all the other areas. While it is unlikely that language learners develop their proficiency along the lines of the 'four skills' identified by the psychometric school, the suggestion that different aspects of proficiency cannot be discerned or developed to different degrees runs contrary to most language teaching experience. All in all, the UCH is not totally convincing and the looseness of the arguments and terminology used cannot entirely disguise the implausibility of the conclusions.

## 5.2.3  The end of the UCH

But what of the statistical evidence for the UCH? Surely the high intercorrelations of cloze and dictations and the factor-analytic studies were incontrovertible proof of the existence of a common factor? Well, yes and no. The significance of the factor-analytic results was reduced somewhat when some of the techniques used and the interpretations made of the results were shown to be questionable.

The debate was lengthy and complex and a detailed rehearsal of the arguments is beyond the scope of this book (details are contained in Oller (1983) and Hughes and Porter (1983)) but the following points emerged:

— the use of Principal Component Analysis (see section 4.8.3) was very likely to produce a large first factor whatever the structure of the data. It was not therefore appropriate to use the technique in order to demonstrate the unitary nature of language proficiency. Most of the early results supporting the UCH were obtained using this method.

— failure to distinguish between PCA and Principal Factor Analysis led to the use of procedures which were not strictly legitimate and produced artificially high results.

— the similarity of the tests used, particularly in the early work, and the frequent absence of an oral test produced an artificially high first factor probably attributable to 'method'.

— the deliberate selection of test populations with a wide proficiency range led to high correlations and a large first factor.

— reanalysis of Oller's data by other workers frequently produced less spectacular results.

The factorial analysis results are not conclusive then. That still leaves the correlation data to be explained. Why should there be such high intercorrelations between 'pragmatic' tests such as cloze and dictation?. One possible explanation is that these tests require the exercise of a wide range of unspecific (and possibly unspecifiable) skills and knowledge. Individual differences along specific parameters will tend to be concealed. We can illustrate this by an analogy.

Suppose we wanted to assess the general health of a number of elderly people. We might decide to eschew orthodox measures such as blood pressure and height/weight ratio and use instead some 'pragmatic' tests such as a one-mile run or gymnastic exercises. These techniques would certainly give information about the health of the testees and there would probably be quite a high correlation between the results of the run and those of the gymnastics. It would clearly be absurd to conclude, however, that 'Health is unitary' on the basis of this statistic.

The fact is that there are various aspects to 'Health' and medical science has developed an explanatory framework which relates them to performance, and procedures (such as blood-tests) for measuring them. Procedures which measure these aspects in isolation are preferred by doctors because they permit diagnosis whereas a bad running performance could be due to a variety of problems. There is, as yet, no similarly well-developed theory which describes language proficiency and relates its structure to performance in the way medical science does. It seems unreasonable, though, to proceed as if no analysis were possible at all and to base all educational and occupational decision-making on cloze and dictation tests in which analysis and sampling are completely absent. It might be pointed out that analysis plays little part in direct performance-referenced tests either, but in this case the purpose of the test is to provide information about some relevant future performance. It is difficult to imagine which future performance restoring deleted text could be relevant to, while taking dictation could only be used in a test for secretaries. Does this mean that dictation and cloze tests are of no interest to the language tester at all? Not necessarily. There are purposes for which these tests are suited. Later we will examine some of their possible uses.

# 5.3 The structure of language proficiency – after the UCH

As well as a great deal of research into the behaviour of cloze and dictation tests, the other legacy of the UCH was considerable confusion about modelling second-language proficiency. The work of Oller and others showed that the dimensions of proficiency adopted by the psychometric testers could not have psychological reality; at the same time, the one-dimensional structure postulated by Oller was shown to be mistaken. The practice of pouring the results from test batteries into powerful number-crunching programs in the hope of something enlightening emerging, was generally discredited. All in all, the dispute left a theoretical and methodological vacuum in its wake.

The question of the structure of language proficiency is an important one for test constructors who use a system-referenced approach: if the derivation of the criterion proficiency from 'the language' is done using an analysis which is inadequate, this threatens the construct validity of the resultant test. Since there is no generally accepted credible model of second-language proficiency (the psychometric model continues to be used in spite of its revealed deficiencies), the validity of all system-referenced tests is questionable in this sense.

The final evidence of the UCH dispute pointed towards the 'partially divisible' nature of language proficiency: while there appeared to be a strong common factor underlying scores on different kinds of language test, this factor did not account for all the variance. Other factors had to be postulated to account for this although they did not often 'make sense' in terms of normal linguistic categories. Tests which did not seem to have very much in common often appeared to load heavily on the same factor. All in all the results of these studies were not very revealing and the idea of a 'partially divisible' language proficiency gives no indication as to what these minor factors might be or how they relate to the common factor or each other.

One possibility which is being investigated is that of a hierarchical relationship between factors (Sang *et al.*, 1986) in which lower-level factors such as pronunciation, lexical knowledge, etc., contribute to intermediate-level factors such as reading ability, which in turn are implicated in the ability to perform more time-constrained top-level tasks such as understanding the pragmatic content of utterances. Sang's model has been shown to be comptabile with data from large-scale studies of German school students.

The working-out of an adequate model for second-language proficiency is still in its early stages. Prerequisites for such a model are an understanding of the contribution that the format of the test makes to the results (the so-called 'method' effect) and the development of test types which probe a wide range of knowledge and skills including the ability to use language in time-constrained oral/aural activities – too often absent from research test batteries in the past. The development of such a model and the resultant language testing rationale could introduce a new era of legitimacy for system-referenced testing.

# 5.4  The use of cloze and dictation tests

We have seen that cloze and dictation tests tend to fall between two stools as far as relevance and applicability are concerned: they cannot be regarded as direct tests since the test performances involved (gap filling, etc.) are not sufficiently similar to any criterion performances which we would normally be interested in. At the same time the lack of analysis and sampling means that they do not meet the requirements for valid indirect tests. They can only be regarded as valid tests if we subscribe to the view that language proficiency is unitary in structure and therefore does not need analysis or sampling. As we have seen, this is not an acceptable assumption for most purposes. The exit test for a language course, for instance, must be based on proper sampling of the course content; the cloze test does not permit the test designer to control content sufficiently to satisfy this requirement.

Nevertheless, there are times when we may be interested in assessing language proficiency in a general way and not worrying too much about its structure or the content of the test. The placement of learners in a general language instruction programme is such an application. The characteristics of placement tests are discussed in detail in Chapter 7 but here we can note that an important function of a placement test is to make an estimate of a learner's general mastery of the language system and to discriminate well between candidates with respect to this characteristic. A properly constructed cloze test of sufficient length will perform just this function. Dictation tests can give information about a wider range of features including listening skills, which may be important in placing learners in classes where the target language will be the language of instruction.

The advantage of these tests over other formats is that they are fairly easy to construct (compared with discrete-point tests) and can be assessed in a fairly 'objective' manner (unlike free-writing or interview performances). Both tests tend to behave quite well statistically providing the texts on which they are based match the proficiency range of the population to be tested. As long as the purpose for which they are used does not require content validity or diagnostic information, then the two techniques are useful and easily administered general language tests.

## 5.4.1 Using cloze tests in practice

### Choosing a text

There has been a lot of controversy about what kind of contextual clues assist a testee to complete a cloze test. Much research has been done to investigate early claims that testees used constraints operating across long stretches of text in order to fill in blanks. While this is theoretically possible, more recent research has shown that candidates tend to use much shorter-range syntactic clues and the effect of wider linguistic context is not as significant as was previously thought. Nevertheless, experience shows that cloze tests work better if the original texts do not deal with topics extraneous to the candidate's experience, preventing them from gaining an overall understanding of the content. The difficulty level of the chosen text should be such that it would be easy to read for the candidates at the top of the anticipated ability range.

As far as length is concerned, the longer a test is, the greater its reliability. Five-hundred words is often quoted as a minimum. This must be set against administrative concerns (time for candidates to complete the test, time spent marking, etc.). Another consideration is that where the decision to be made is relatively crude (e.g. the placement of learners in two or three proficiency groups) great sensitivity in the placement test is not required and 200 words is probably sufficient.

### Deletion frequency

We can either delete selected words or delete words at regular intervals (every seventh word is often chosen). Tests in which selected words have been deleted (e.g. grammatically significant words) have not been shown to be superior in performance to tests where a regular deletion-interval has been used. This demonstrates once more that performance on these tests is not closely determined by 'content' as constituted by the deleted items. A typical test will consist of a first sentence left intact, deletions at regular intervals throughout the body of the text and an intact stretch at the end.

### Marking the test

There are two ways of marking the test. We may accept as correct only the original word or we may take any 'acceptable' word as being correct. The 'exact' scoring method has the advantage of being simple enough to be used by an unqualified person with a key to the items. The 'acceptable' method requires interpretation by the scorer as to which responses count as 'acceptable', although a closed list for each blank can be compiled by giving the test to a group of native speakers. While the two methods have been shown to give quite highly correlated results, the 'exact' method tends to depress the scores (since many of the top candidates' perfectly good responses are counted as incorrect). This results in a smaller spread of scores. If the aim is to discriminate among candidates, then the test must be made longer to achieve the same numerical separation. For this reason the 'acceptable' method is usually adopted for most purposes.

Research has also been done into spelling. The best policy is to accept a response if it is recognizable. If information about a candidate's spelling is required, this is best obtained through a specifically written test.

## 5.5  Using dictation

Although administratively more demanding, dictation tests can assess a wider range of features than cloze tests.

Like the cloze test, the text used for dictation should be easily understood by candidates at the top of the proficiency range, when read at normal speed. Esoteric topics should be avoided.

The most satisfactory way of administering the test is to give three readings, the first and third at normal speed and the second at dictation speed (sentence fragments – not individual words).

To ensure uniformity the text can be recorded beforehand and played back at a number of different administrations. This also allows individual candidates to be tested one at a time using headphones when group administration is not possible.

Marking schemes for dictation can be very elaborate though there is probably little to be gained from sophisticated systems. The simplest method is to subtract one from the total number of words for each word which is unrecognizable or missing. Spelling is ignored, as in cloze testing, though it may be decided to penalize spelling mistakes which are also structural errors:

He clean it everyday*

Used in this way, cloze and dictation tests can provide reliable estimates of general language proficiency where content validity or relationship to a criterion performance are not important and the subsequent decisions will not be particularly subtle.

# 6

# Performance-referenced and task-based test designs

The last few chapters have dealt with the kind of tests which we have decided to call system-referenced: they are designed to evaluate language mastery as a psychological construct without specific reference to any particular use of it. The quarrel between Oller and the psychometric theorists was about the *nature* of this construct: neither side doubted that this generalized, psychological proficiency was the proper target of testing techniques.

During the 1970s in Britain and Europe, interest grew in 'starting at the other end' and developing tests which assessed the candidate's ability to perform some specific task using the language. There had always been an established tradition of this kind of testing for occupational or vocational purposes, but in the field of language testing the availability of linguistic analysis as a basis for test construction provided a more attractive alternative to task-based design methods.

It will be recalled that Lado's objection to this approach (quoted in full in section 3.2.2.) was that the situations in which language is used are too various to be effectively sampled for test construction purposes, while language elements are more limited in number. It is therefore more effective to sample the elements rather than the situations and the resulting test will have greater validity. There is certainly some truth in this assertion but two later developments made the sampling of situations of use more feasible and more desirable.

The first was the advent of 'notional-functional' syllabuses. The idea of classifying language elements in terms of what a speaker can do using them led to the construction of inventories of 'discourse functions'. This development seemed to offer the possibility of a systematic approach to sampling the purposes for which language is used and thus to a rationale for a different kind of language test: one which would specify the criterion performance in terms of what the candidate could do rather than in terms of the systemic elements which had been mastered. (As we shall see later, the difficulties of this, while not insuperable as Lado thought, are still formidable.) At the same time, the increasing use of notional-functional terminology in describing course objectives led to an awareness of a certain mismatch between the content of such courses and the tests available for evaluating their outcome.

The second development was the interest in teaching language to groups of learners with specific purposes, e.g. doctors or sales representatives. The design of such courses typically starts by looking at the (by definition) limited range of situations and activities for which the instruction will prepare the learners (conducting medical examinations, making appointments over the phone, etc). This analysis can then be used as a basis for the design of the course and also that of the exit test. In this case the results of the test can be used to predict the candidates' ability to use the language for the purposes specified in the description of the course objectives. Again it is important not to underestimate the difficulties, both practical and theoretical, which are involved in this apparently straightforward procedure. Nevertheless, the existence of courses for learners with fairly specific foreseeable needs, does create a need for evaluation that cannot be satisfactorily met by test types based on a narrowly systemic view of the performance targets. At best the use of such tests will not permit confident predictions about learner's future performance. At the worst the 'washback' effect may lead to 'teaching for the exam' so that the carefully researched course objectives may become supplanted by systemic considerations.

For these two reasons then, recent developments in language testing have been concerned with the problems of producing tests which reflect innovations in language teaching and research, whilst at the same time retaining the traditional virtues of validity and reliability. A variety of terms has been used for such tests of which 'communicative' is probably the least helpful. Since two contrasting tendencies can be discerned among tests of this kind we shall distinguish between tests which are strictly performance-referenced and those which are merely task-based.

A direct performance-referenced test involves near-simulation of some future or potential activity and results of the test can be used to predict the candidate's ability to perform that or similar tasks in the future. 'Similar' here can be interpreted with varying degrees of liberality. If the decision which the test must facilitate depends crucially on the ability of the candidate to perform precisely the tasks which constitute the test performance (e.g. a driving test) then the test is rigorously performance-referenced. If, however, the relevant future tasks cannot be specified exactly or are only vaguely related to the test performance then the results of the test are only evidence of a general ability to perform tasks of that type. In this case we may call the test 'task-based' in recognition of the fact that it involves doing something which looks like a fairly authentic example of language use, although we are not specifically interested in the ability of the candidate to perform precisely that task. The test provides evidence of 'abilities' which may be transferable to other task types. This is clearly a matter of degree: at one extreme are strictly performance-referenced tests like driving tests; at the other are system-referenced tests, in which the apparently 'authentic' language task in the test is merely a pretext for eliciting a performance from the candidate which will give evidence of the most generalizable type of ability, i.e. language proficiency.

Two quite different tests in this sense may use the same task; the difference in the designer's focus is revealed by the approach to assessment of the performance.

Thus, a test which involved preparing a report from a source-file may form part of a performance-referenced test for candidates who will have to prepare reports in the future. On the other hand, if the report-writing activity is merely a way of giving an air of 'authenticity' to what is essentially a test of general writing ability, then it is a task-based test. The task itself may be identical but the measurement and judgement will be different. For instance, deficiencies of presentation which may be judged serious in the work of a potential report-writer, may be overlooked if the test is merely one of general writing ability to which conventions of report presentation are too specialized to be relevant.

Figures 6.1 and 6.2 provide another illustration of this distinction. Both are tests of listening. The first involves compiling a reply to a telex following spoken instructions. Since it comes from the 'RSA Certificate in EFL for Secretaries' it can be considered a fairly performance-referenced test: the task is relevant to future performance. The second (taken from the 'RSA Test in the Communicative Use of English') involves listening to a telephone conversation and correcting an advertisement. While conceivably something which a language learner might have to do, the task is not so readily identified with some future performance and is really a general test of listening.

Genuinely performance-referenced tests are not common among public examinations. University entrance tests such as the British Council ELTS test are among

---

QUESTION TWO

LOOK AT THE TELEX BELOW. LISTEN TO MR POINTER'S INSTRUCTIONS ON THE TAPE. MAKE NOTES IF YOU WANT TO. THEN WRITE A SUITABLE TELEX IN REPLY IN THE SPACE AT THE BOTTOM OF THE PAGE.

```
27/07/88 14:49
Telex line  1 - Message RE0306 received at 27/07/88 14:48

265806 EDWARD G
885887 HODDER G


ATTN. : MR. POINTER

PLEASE CONFIRM ARRIVAL AIRPORT FRIDAY.   TIME AND FLIGHT.
WILL ARRANGE TO MEET.

LESIEUR


885887 HODDER G
```

---

When you've finished typing that report I wonder if you could just send a short telex back to Pierre Lesieur in Paris giving him details of my travel plans next Friday. I'm catching Flight No BA 774 and it'll be arriving at 14.35 Paris local time. Can you make sure it goes off today.

---

Fig 6.1

---

TELEPHONE

1.  Find the mistakes in this advertisement. Put a ring (O) round any information that is different from what you hear. (Example: Wednesday: 6.00 pm)

DON'T MISS
HARLEM GLOBETROTTERS
with their
GREAT FOOTBALL DISPLAY
at
WEMBLEY ARENA

Saturday: 7.30 p.m.
Sunday: 3.30 and 6.30 p.m.
(and all of next week)

Seats: £2 and £5.50
(half price for children)

---

Fig 6.2

the few examples. Populations of candidates sharing specific performance goals are usually too small to justify the development of specific exams of this type. In spite of this, the bulk of this chapter will be concerned with performance-referenced tests in the specific sense, both because of their importance in instructional programmes and also because task-based tests can be considered as being derived from them by the relaxation of rigorous specificity requirements.

# 6.1 Economy and comparability – drawbacks of performance-referenced testing

One of the advantages of the system-referenced test which measures mastery of the elements of the language, is that while the results cannot be directly extrapolated to a particular performance, they are vaguely relevant to a wide range of needs and situations. Since performance-referenced tests are more limited in the applicability of their results there have to be more of them – with a consequent increase in the cost and time required for development. A comparison between the American university placement test, the TOEFL (one form of the test, all candidates sit it) and the British council ELTS test (some sections have half-a-dozen versions depending on the future study area of the candidate) shows that there is a price to pay if we want finely tuned tests.

The second problem, that of comparability, concerns the need to establish some kind of equivalence between the results of different kinds of test. Does a pass on an English exam for doctors indicate a higher or lower level than a pass on an English exam for bilingual secretaries? Strictly speaking of course, the question is non-sensical; we may as well ask if a life-saving certificate is more advanced than a diploma in shorthand: the two criteria are not comparable outside their own domains. Nevertheless, it is understandable that there should be concern that results on parallel modules of the ELTS test, say, are comparable and that candidates who do the Technology Section are not getting an 'easy ride' compared to those doing Social Sciences. This can be checked by mapping results onto a common scale of language mastery (see section 6.3.4) although this practice to some extent runs counter to the general philosophy of the test.

It is clear then that the move towards greater specificity involved in the development of performance-referenced tests has its drawbacks. Whether the advantages gained from the (potentially) greater validity of such tests outweigh these disadvantages will obviously depend on the nature of the decisions to be made on the basis of the test results and how costly mistakes will be.

## 6.2  The development of direct performance-referenced tests

A distinction was made in Chapter 2 between direct and indirect tests on the basis of how similar the test performance was to the future or potential performance which the test has been designed to give information about. In direct tests, involving little analysis, the test performance is very similar to the criterion performance and the test may be regarded as a near-simulation of the criterion activity. The driving test is a test of this kind. In the field of language testing, examples include simulated oral interaction, writing assignments and information retrieval tasks of various kinds. Before we look at the design procedure in detail let us re-examine the model in order to identify the key features of the approach.

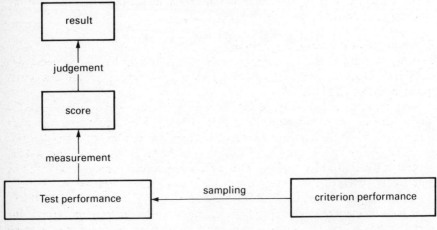

Fig 6.3

Starting by establishing the criterion performance (say, making a business trip abroad), by a process of sampling, a series of key activities are identified (hiring a car, booking a hotel room, etc.). A simulation is set up in which the candidate is required to perform one of the activities with suitable interlocutors pretending to be receptionists, etc. The candidate's performance is assessed in one of a number of ways which we shall go into later and a score is arrived at. Finally a judgement must be made as to whether the score is sufficiently high to constitute a pass. Obviously this will depend on the purpose of the test, i.e. what sort of decision has to be made and how much margin for error needs to be left. The outcome of the judgement produces the result.

All of these stages have associated difficulties, some of them quite severe. Let us examine them:

## 6.2.1 Sampling the criterion performance – choosing the tasks

In its extreme form, the direct approach to performance-referenced testing involves simulating a 'slice of life' and seeing how well the candidate fares. Since the design of the test procedure involves little analysis of the criterion performance but merely seeks to replicate it, this approach sidesteps problems of identifying relevant dimensions of the criterion performance. It is generally not difficult to predict or discover through investigation the kinds of activities which the candidate will be engaged in; the problems are mainly administrative in finding time and personnel to simulate a reasonable sample of these situations. Whilst a paper-and-pencil test can be administered and scored in a couple of hours by one unqualified person to several dozen candidates, even the simplest oral interactive test, such as the face-to-face interview, requires at least ten minutes of a trained interviewer's time per candidate. If we add a separate assessor to the interview situation (which substantially increases the reliability of the procedure), the resource requirements are even higher. This has to be weighed against possible advantages in validity of such test procedures and the importance of the decisions which must be made.

### Examples of oral interactive formats

In order to examine the key features of these sort of tests let us examine a few techniques which can be used. (A practical look at a wide range of procedures can be found in Carroll and Hall, 1984.)

Since these are all role-plays of some kind in which the candidate is required to play a part, an important principle is that the candidate should be given clear instructions and sufficient time to understand them. The validity of the test depends on the candidate's understanding of the nature of the task to be carried out and the context in which it will take place. This usually requires a 'waiting-room' of some kind (more resources!), where the candidate can prepare himself for the test. Alternatively, use can be made of the 'resources-pack' (Carroll and Hall, 1985). This is a collection of texts, illustrations and maps which will form the basis of the text activities. The candidate is given sufficient time to familiarize himself completely with the materials (perhaps even taking them home overnight). In this way, possible distortions of the results due to differences in familiarity with the topics of the test are minimized.

*(1) The face-to-face interview*
In its classical form the interview was merely a way of getting a sample of language out of the candidate so that it could be assessed for formal acceptability. This made it strictly a system-referenced test. If the interview is structured, however, and the candidate has a task to perform, then the procedure can provide hard evidence about future performance. An example which has been used to appoint overseas graduate students as teaching assistants in American universities is the 'mini-tutorial'. A candidate is given a list of key terms in his subject discipline and must prepare to explain one of these, using a blackboard if he wishes, to an interlocutor who pretends to be a freshman student. The reliability of these procedures can be increased by having the assessment made by an observer who does not take part in the interaction.

*(ii) Pair assessment*
In this kind of test candidates are given a task which can only be carried out by co-operating with another candidate. For example, two candidates may have to prepare an itinerary. One has a map and the other has train and bus timetables. During their discussion the performances are assessed by an observer. Although it might seem that this procedure could lead to domination of the exchange by one candidate, in practice this rarely happens, possibly because each candidate realizes that the other's contribution is necessary for him to exhibit his own ability. This method has the advantage that the relationship between the candidate and the interlocutor is more balanced than in the interview, where the interviewer is inevitably seen as a kind of inquisitor. Since two candidates are assessed at the same time there is a resultant saving in time and personnel. A disadvantage of the method is that the interaction cannot be guided by the examiner as in an interview, and the task and instructions must be very carefully designed to elicit the desired perform-ance from the candidate. In practice it is very difficult to determine in advance which sort of formats will 'work' for pair assessment and there is no substitute for extensive piloting and refinement of promising task types.

*(iii) Group assessment*
The extreme form of this kind of test format is the group assessment in which the performances of a number of candidates are assessed during an extended role-play. A useful technique is the 'tribunal' simulation in which half the group are members of a board which must make some kind of decision, e.g. about allocating low-rent housing to deserving families. The other half of the group plays the families applying for the housing. The simulation has three stages. In the first stage the 'families' examine their case histories and decide how to present their appeal. At the same time the tribunal looks at the description of the housing and decides on criteria for allocation. In the second phase each family presents its case and is questioned by the tribunal. In the last phase the tribunal discusses the merit of the families and reaches a conclusion. Certain devices can be built in to ensure participation by all candi-dates: each member of the panel may be told secretly that they have a special interest in one of the families receiving the housing and must therefore question them sympathetically and push their case during the discussion. The performances are assessed by one or more observers who move from group to group during the simulation.

One of the advantages of this technique is that, although it takes over an hour, it can be used with twelve or more candidates, thus being fairly economical in terms of time. Another positive point is that, since each candidate can be assessed after speaking for a period of time, 'warm-up' problems are avoided and the assessor sees the candidates after they have got into their stride. It can also be quite an enjoyable activity (though this is not normally thought of as being important in a testing technique!).

Group assessment also has several disadvantages. As in pair assessment, the examiner cannot directly intervene to guide the course of the proceedings. This means that the task must be carefully designed to ensure that it works smoothly and that all candidates have a chance to produce a properly assessable performance. A second drawback is that the roles of the participants are not all the same. In our example some of the candidates are committee members and some are housing applicants. If our test is a strictly performance-referenced one, i.e. it is supposed to give information about a particular performance (say, to assess ability to conduct interviews) then it is only valid for some of the candidates: those who formed part of the committee. The performances of the other candidates will not be strictly relevant to the assessment. If, on the other hand, the test is more task-based (in the sense identified above), then the assessor will be looking for features of the performances which can be generalized to a range of different situations. In this case the difference between the two kinds of role may not be so important.

### The mirage of 'authenticity'
The growth in popularity of these kinds of test over recent years has sometimes given rise to discussion of how 'authentic' such procedures can be. Often the suggestion has been that the validity of the procedures is crucially dependent on their authenticity and that it is therefore sufficient to demonstrate the inauthenticity of a technique to call its validity into question. Part of the problem stems from confusion about the relationship between validity and authenticity.

The first thing which needs to be made clear is that any activity which takes place for the purposes of assessment is, by necessity, inauthentic. The call for authenticity in language testing tasks is therefore futile; the only procedure which could satisfy this requirement would involve the assessor following the testee around as he goes about his daily business. This is sometimes called 'direct assessment' and is very costly and rarely feasible. All other test tasks differ from their real-life equivalents in that the intentions of the person performing them are radically altered by the fact that he is doing a test.

The man at the Hertz counter wants to rent a car. The man at the simulated Hertz counter has no interest in renting a car although he must feign this intention. At the same time he must conceal his real intention, which is to exhibit his language abilities in the best possible light for the examiner. The candidate's activity is a 'performance' in the theatrical sense of the word. In pair or group assessment this is even more the case: the candidates are engaged in a co-operative venture whose aim is to 'put on a show' for the assessor.

Earlier (2.2.1) we identified the degree of similarity between test and criterion performance as the chief factor determining how valid the test was i.e. how confidently decisions could be based on the results. In the car-rental example, the test procedure differs from the criterion procedure in that as well as renting a car, the candidate must also play a role. Does this render illegitimate our extrapolation from the test performance to criterion performance? Two points of view are possible here. It might be maintained that a candidate's inability to play out a particular part in a test simulation (due say, to lack of imagination or excessive nervousness) is not grounds for thinking that he could not have performed the task in real life. If this is true, then the validity of the test is compromised to some extent.

On the other hand it may be pointed out that there is a dramaturgical dimension to all interpersonal exchanges (especially when using a foreign tongue) and that analysis of social relations in such terms reveals the centrality of role-playing activities to all social interaction (Goffman, 1959). From this point of view the differences between the demands made on the candidate by the test procedure and the real-life situation are less marked: both require him to adopt a role in order to carry out the task. The dispute about authenticity then boils down to this: no test procedure can ever be fully authentic since it inevitably involves role-playing on the part of the testee. On the other hand, this is an aspect of real-life use of language and its presence in the test situation may therefore be less of a problem than it seems at first. It is interesting that formats such as 'tribunals' of the kind described above lend themselves well to testing purposes; perhaps because even in real life their theatrical structure requires role-playing from the participants and this encourages the testees to recognize and exploit this dramatic potential during the test.

### Direct performance-referenced writing tests

As well as tests of oral interaction, it is possible to devise tests which assess the ability to carry out tasks using writing skills. These tests are generally more economical to administer since many candidates can do the test at the same time and their texts can be assessed later. Tasks can range from the very simple, such as writing a telephone message from the text of a telephone call, to much more ambitious, such as preparing a report after detailed study of a case-file. (Again, Carroll and Hall, 1985 contains details of possible formats.)

Information for writing tasks can be presented using recorded texts. Though care is needed here. When someone is listening to important information, they are usually in a position to ask for repetition or clarification from the speaker. Exceptions to this (university lectures and airport announcements) are few. This is obviously not possible with a tape-recorder and the validity of the test procedure can be compromised if we use recorded information of a kind which is usually transferred face-to-face. The ability to perform specific tasks which involve listening (as opposed to general listening ability) is best assessed through oral-interactional formats.

## 6.2.2  Measuring the direct test performance

Having found a way of eliciting the performance from the candidate, we must now measure it. This means effectively that a score or scores must be assigned which will form the basis for the judgement. It is in precisely this area where task-based tests make most demands on the ingenuity of the test designer. The direct test performance has all the open-endedness and unpredictability which characterizes normal language use. These features are often held up as being the advantages of this approach. At the same time however they are what makes the performance very difficult to measure in comparison with a paper-and-pencil test or other indirect procedure.

Various ways of making the measurement are possible:

## 1. The 'simple success' criterion

If our test is of the strictly performance-referenced type and we are only interested in whether the candidate will be able to produce the criterion performance then we can award one of two scores: successful or unsuccessful. Either the car-hire candidate succeeded in hiring the correct car for the correct period or he did not. If we are specifically interested in a candidate's immediate car-hiring ability this is a reasonable approach.

## 2. Band descriptor scales

On the other hand we may want to know **how** successful or unsuccessful he was (possibly for purposes of remedial instruction). In this case we can make use of a scale showing various degrees of success:

| | |
|---|---|
| 4 | car hired without any difficulty |
| 3 | car hired with occasional breakdowns in communication |
| 2 | car hired but considerable help was required from interlocutor |
| 1 | candidate failed to hire car in spite of help from interlocutor |
| 0 | candidate almost entirely unable to indicate requirements |

Fig 6.4

This scale permits comparisons between candidates as well as giving some idea of where a performance lies in absolute terms.

The use of scales such as this is not recent. The American Foreign Service Institute (FSI) has used scales to assess the interview performance of employees since just after the war. A total of five different scales is used: Accent. Grammar, Fluency, Vocabulary and Comprehension.

It will be noted, however, that the features which are assessed are almost exclusively linguistic and indeed, in the scales themselves, there is little reference to any features of the performance beyond the speed and correctness of the language. This places the test well towards the system-referenced end of the continuum. Scales making reference to what is actually achieved by the candidate are a comparatively more recent development.

In considering multi-band scales we come up against a central problem in task-based assessment – unreliability. With the two-band scale described above there was little to discuss. Two assessors would be unlikely to disagree since the success or otherwise of the candidate's attempt to hire a car is plain to see.

With five levels of descriptors there is more room for disagreement and the possibility that two assessors might assign a performance to different bands becomes more of a problem. We will look at this sort of unreliability and how it can be minimized a little later.

## More general scales

The scale reproduced above is only suitable for assessing one kind of performance – that of hiring a car. It would have to be modified if it were used with another type of task.

For reasons of economy and comparability we can employ more general scales which can be used to assess a wider range of interaction tasks. The following scale is among those used in the British Council ELTS test to assess performance during the structured interview. (Fig. 6.5)

Clearly the descriptors are relevant to any type of interview situation since they refer to the candidate's ability to manage the exchange in a general way without referring to any particular task which is carried out. In this sense their greater generality places the test a little more towards the system-referenced end of the scale though not as far as the FSI scales whose criteria are almost exclusively linguistic.

## Multidimensional scales

Once we go beyond simple 'task-success' in our assessment of the test performance then we have to recognize that there may be several aspects of the performance which merit assessment. We may want to measure how much contribution the candidate makes to the exchange, how independent of the interlocutor he is as well as more traditional features such as accuracy and speed. Figure 6.6. shows an expansion of level 5.5 of the ELTS interview scale to describe the performance in more detail.

This expansion adds precision to the band descriptor but introduces two problems. One is that these dimensions of the performance are not necessarily correlated so that a performance may be band 7.0 as far as its appropriacy is concerned but band 5.0 in terms of flexibility. It is not clear what this would mean. The other problem is that the expanded descriptors are obviously too unwieldy to be used in the heat of a real assessment. They should perhaps be regarded more as instruments for the construction of the abbreviated scales.

## The construction and use of scales

To be useful, an assessment scale should satisfy two requirements:

Firstly the performance features it describes it should be of relevance to the success of the criterion performance. The FSI scales described above have been criticized because the features they describe (grammatical accuracy, accent, etc.) are not obviously relatable to what the candidate is supposed to be able to do (described in some detail elsewhere in the specification).

Secondly the description of the features must allow the assessor to readily identify them in the candidate's performance. 'Candidate participates with confidence.' is not something that is immediately observable during the performance. 'Candidate frequently initiates during the exchange.' is far easier to decide about.

Considerable work goes into the preparation and refinement of assessment scales. This work is extremely important since it is precisely in the area of

## 2 Interview assessment scale
Band

| | |
|---|---|
| 9 | **Expert speaker.** Speaks with authority on a variety of topics. Can initiate, expand and develop a theme. |
| 8 | **Very good non-native speaker.** Maintains effectively his own part of a discussion. Initiates, maintains and elaborates as necessary. Reveals humour where needed and responds to attitudinal tones. |
| 7 | **Good speaker.** Presents case clearly and logically and can develop the dialogue coherently and constructively. Rather less flexible and fluent than Band 8 performer but can respond to main changes of tone or topic. Some hesitation and repetition due to a measure of language restriction but interacts effectively. |
| 6 | **Competent speaker.** Is able to maintain theme of dialogue, to follow topic switches and to use and appreciate main attitude markers. Stumbles and hesitates at times but is reasonably fluent otherwise. Some errors and inappropriate language but these will not impede exchange of views. Shows some independence in discussion with ability to initiate. |
| 5 | **Modest speaker.** Although gist of dialogue is relevant and can be basically understood, there are noticeable deficiencies in mastery of language patterns and style. Needs to ask for repetition or clarification and similarly to be asked for them. Lacks flexibility and initiative. The interviewer often has to speak rather deliberately. Copes but not with great style or interest. |
| 4 | **Marginal speaker.** Can maintain dialogue but in a rather passive manner, rarely taking initiative or guiding the discussion. Has difficulty in following English at normal speed; lacks fluency and probably accuracy in speaking. The dialogue is therefore neither easy nor flowing. Nevertheless, gives the impression that he is in touch with the gist of the dialogue even if not wholly master of it. Marked L1 accent. |
| 3 | **Extremely limited speaker.** Dialogue is a drawn-out affair punctuated with hesitations and misunderstandings. Only catches part of normal speech and unable to produce continuous and accurate discourse. Basic merit is just hanging on to discussion gist, without making major contribution to it. |
| 2 | **Intermittent speaker.** No working facility; occasional, sporadic communication. |
| 1/0 | **Non-speaker.** Not able to understand and/or speak. |

Fig 6.5

measurement that the inadequacies of task-based testing are most evident. The complexity of the behaviour which is elicited by these kinds of procedure makes reliable assessment extremely problematic. A number of measures can be taken to make assessment more reliable.

1 Make the scales themselves explicit and unambiguous and refer to readily observable aspects of the performance.

2 Train all assessors using recordings (video if possible) of sample performances. Do not use assessors whose ratings are not consistent with the consensus.

3 If possible, separate the role of interlocutor and assessor so that assessment can

**5  Oral interaction assessment scale**

Intermediate Level (equivalent to Band 5.5 or 'L' score of 55 minimum)

| | |
|---|---|
| *Size* | Can participate in a discussion with several people keeping in touch with the gist even if occasional lack of grasp of details. |
| *Complexity* | Can understand and discuss one or two major points and supporting details. Can make a firm point but disturbed by noise and distractions. |
| *Range* | Can describe and discuss implications of events, graphics and objects using a number of language skills and tones. |
| *Speed* | Will have breaks in comprehension in normal, rapid speech presentations and his own speech will be of less than native tempo for stretches. |
| *Flexibility* | Can cope with occasional but not frequent switches of topic and style of presentation. Recognizes when a different type of utterance, such as a joke, is being used, and changes his own style accordingly. |
| *Accuracy* | Does not seriously misinterpret overt meaning of utterance but not quite so ready to understand implied meaning. Uses language at his disposal accurately and aware of his usage limitations. Accent and sometimes usage is likely to be patently foreign. |
| *Appropriacy* | Appreciates major styles of presentation including some slang and regional usages, but can be puzzled by such deviations from the norm. Does not always use slang appropriately or adapt style of presentation. |
| *Independence* | Will not often have to ask for clarification unless presentation is unusually rapid or confusing. Can 'speak on his feet' but needs more recourse to preparation and notes than would a fully competent speaker. |
| *Repetition* | May ask for repetition if speech is rapid or extended. |
| *Hesitation* | Prone to more false starts and space-fillers than a fully competent speaker. |
| Overall | *A useful participant in a discussion or interview. Keeps in touch with main points and able to put over his own point of view but level of comprehension and fluency lies between Basic and Advanced level performances.* |

Fig 6.6

take place without the assessor having to manage the interview at the same time.

4  If resources permit, use two or more assessors. Record performances so that 'replays' can be used to settle disputes between assessors.

Using the above techniques, reasonable inter-rater reliability can be achieved. It will always be inferior, however, to that of 'objectively-scored' tests such as multiple-choice. This has to be set against the advantages of using this kind of test, i.e. the greater relevance to the criterion performance.

## 6.2.3  Making the judgement

In measuring the test performance we were concerned about 'how good' it was. In making the judgement we are concerned with deciding if it was 'good enough'. This is the 'pass-mark problem' which we touched upon in section 2.2.1. As we saw earlier, this essentially involves deciding what the scores *mean*. If the test result is to be the basis of a decision, then we need to establish what a candidate with a particular score can actually do. There are three ways in which we can make this connection between the score and the criterion performance.

1 In indirect tests this is often done by the procedure of empirical validation of the kind outlined in 2.2.2 and norm-referencing (see 3.4). In this way we can determine that a score of 65 per cent on the test is sufficient for a particular activity or job.

2 Alternatively, if the test performance has some relation to the criterion performance we can ask some experienced informers to have a look at the test and estimate what sort of score would be sufficient to indicate a satisfactory level of ability. This is often done for occupational tests. An experienced electrical engineer is asked to indicate how well a series of tasks should be performed in order to qualify as a technician of a certain grade.

3 Finally if the test performance is a simulation of the criterion performance then the problem of setting the pass-mark disappears: success in performing the test task directly implies that the performance is satisfactory.

One of the advantages which are claimed for task-based tests is that this derivation of pass-marks by inspection of the test is more feasible because the test performance bears some similarity to the criterion performance. In an indirect test such as multiple-choice it is far more difficult to say what a score means in functional terms. When we can see how difficult a test is just by looking at it we have removed at a stroke, two problems that beset the indirect test constructor: firstly, that of deciding what the pass-mark should be, and secondly, that of maintaining the level of difficulty from administration to administration.

While this is an attractive prospect in theory, in practice, criterion-referencing turns out to be less straightforward than might be expected. Let us look at some examples:

In our car-hire example, if we use a two-band assessment: successful or unsuccessful, then we have an extreme example of a performance-referenced test and we can use method 3 above to set the pass-mark. If we have to decide on the candidate's suitability for a job entirely on the basis of his ability to hire cars (this is rather unlikely of course), then the judgement is already contained in the measurement: successful equals pass; unsuccessful equals fail. The criteria of success for hiring a car are entirely relevant to the test performance and can be used as the basis for arriving at the test result: a clear example of a criterion-referenced test.

If we are using the five-band scale, however, things are a little less clear-cut: there are three grades which describe a successful car-hiring performance. Where do we draw the line between 'good enough' and 'not good enough'? This can only be decided on the basis of the job requirements: if we can't take risks then we only pass candidates with 5. Otherwise we might accept 4 as a pass, or even 3. This is an example of the second procedure described above, using an informed judgement to arrive at a pass-mark. Although the measurement doesn't lead immediately to a judgement as in the two-band scale, our decision can still be made on reasonable grounds just by inspecting the band descriptors. The procedure still enjoys the advantages claimed for criterion-referenced tests in that it is clear what the scores mean and the level of difficulty of the test can be established by inspection.

It is when we move towards measurements based on general assessment scales of the ELTS variety that using criterion-referencing to arrive at a judgement becomes more difficult. The purpose of the ELTS test is to predict the ability of a candidate to follow a course at a British university. The criterion performance is therefore quite complex. The test performance of the candidate may be related to this criterion performance, but the scales make no reference to any specific event or activity type. The descriptors identifying general features of interview performances but criteria of success in specific activities, e.g. tutorials, lab sessions, are absent. To what extent can the connection be made, then, between a candidate's score and his suitability for a particular course? Well, obviously a description, even in fairly general terms, is better than a bald numerical score. If we are considering candidates for an MSc. course in Civil Engineering then we can safely exclude candidates scoring 4 or below while performances at bands 8 and 9 definitely look acceptable. That still leaves levels 5, 6, and 7. There is simply no principled way of deciding where to insert the cut-off point among these bands because the descriptions do not refer specifically to the criterion performance. This is inevitable: the test must give information relevant to a large number of different institutions and courses. At the same time it must be economical in terms of time.

What happens in practice in the ELTS test is that the candidate's performance is reported as scores on five bands (corresponding to the different parts of the test). This 'profile' is then checked against the 'profile' of the proposed university course which indicates the minimum score on each band which is acceptable (see Fig. 6.7).

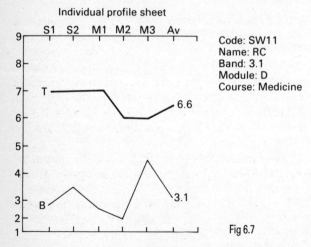

Fig 6.7

If the course profile does not exceed the candidate's profile then the candidate can be accepted. The question is, where do these course profiles come from? Who decides what are the minimum scores on each band necessary to follow a particular course? In theory the profiles should be derived from observation of students on these courses in order to specify the demands which their studies make on their language resources. This is very time-consuming however, and in practice the profiles were arrived at by looking at course materials and consultation with academic staff and English-teaching staff responsible for preparing students for these courses. Use has to be made of the idea of a 'typical' Business Studies Course, for example and this rather detracts from the value of the test instrument. The making of the judgement in the ELTS test, then, is accomplished by technique 2 above. Unlike the technician's test, however, the complexity and variability of the criterion performance make this look rather less attractive as a way of setting a standard. Technique 1 (empirical validation) is not really feasible since to be done properly it would involve allowing candidates to start their courses even though their test scores seemed to indicate unsuitability.

Thus we can see that the need for generality in the ELTS test prevents it from enjoying the ease of pass-mark setting which a more performance-referenced test (e.g. the car-hire example) can achieve. In this respect the ELTS is no different from any other kind of public language test. The problem is a general one and can be summarized thus: if a test is to be relevant to a large-enough audience to justify the time and money spent on its development, its procedures and measurements cannot be specific to one set of criterion performances. In generalizing away from specific performances, however, the meanings of the scores in operational terms and the judgements based upon them become less determinate and the setting of pass-marks more problematical.

Any solution found to this problem must be a compromise.

# 6.3 Indirect performance-referenced tests

Now we turn to an approach to test-construction which, while taking some future or potential performance as its criterion, makes use of an analytical procedure to derive an underlying proficiency. The extent to which this is done is, of course, a matter of degree. Even in those test types which we have chosen to call 'direct', a certain amount of analysis must be performed for sampling purposes (the driving examiner needs his checklist of tasks) or in order to define the criterion. Nevertheless we can usefully distinguish between this kind of minimal analysis which is forced on the test designer and the kind of analysis which produced a test design in which test and criterion performance are quite different.

The model for this kind of test construction resembles that of the direct test except that between the test and criterion performance are now interposed the two intermediate constructs of criterion and test proficiency. The criterion proficiency, it will be recalled, is what the testee has to know or be able to do in order to produce the criterion performance. The test proficiency is a sample of this and is what the testee must know or be able to do in order to produce the test performance.

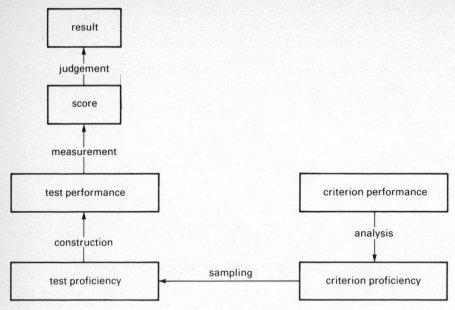

Fig 6.8

Although the test and criterion performance may be very different, the results of the test are still judged to be relevant providing the various stages of analysis, sampling and construction have been carried out properly. Since this is frequently open to doubt, the validity of the test will usually have to be confirmed through empirical validation of some sort as described in section 2.2.2.

We shall now look in detail at the stages involved in the construction of an indirect performance-referenced test. A number of examples will be used but since the most ambitious test of this kind to emerge in recent years is the British Council ELTS test, particular reference will be made to the principles involved in its construction. A hypothetical 'slice' out of the test construction was shown in Figure 2.10 illustrating the possible derivation of one item in a sub-test from part of the description of the criterion performance.

## 6.3.1  Analysis of the criterion performance

Taking apart a language performance in order to identify its relevant parameters is no easy matter. At the beginning of the 60s Robert Lado declared it impossible owing to problems of description and sampling. Nearly thirty years later the development of new models and tools in the social and linguistic sciences have made it more feasible.

Certainly the most ambitious attempt to characterize the knowledge and skills required for a language user in a particular context was Munby's model described in 'Communicative Syllabus Design' (Munby, 1978). Using a synthesis of linguistic and sociolinguistic frameworks he identified a number of parameters in terms of which communicative events and acts could be described in great detail. The original purpose of this work was to provide a methodical procedure for identifying the content of ESP syllabuses through a consideration of what the learner would need to do with the language, with whom, in what context, and with what degree of adequacy.

Thus, in order to construct an ESP course for waiters the following aspects would be considered:

| | |
|---|---|
| THE LEARNER | – the personal details of the participant (age, etc.) |
| THE PURPOSE | – why the language is needed (dealing with English speaking clients) |
| THE DOMAIN | – where and when the language will be used (restaurant) |
| INTERACTION | – who it will be used with and their relationship with the learner (clients, colleagues, boss) |
| INSTRUMENTALITY | – medium (speech) and channel (face to face) |
| DIALECT | – the variety produced and understood (Standard British and American English) |
| LEVEL | – what standard of performance is required (described by various scales) |
| EVENTS and ACTIVITIES | – detailed kinds of interaction and situation. |
| ATTITUDINAL TONE | – the tones the learner must be able to convey and recognize (polite, formal, etc.). |
| FUNCTIONS | – the microfunctions necessary to perform in the situations identified in the above analysis (directing, recommending, etc.) |
| LANGUAGE SKILLS | – The detailed skills enabling performance of the necessary microfunctions. |

For each of these parameters Munby provides an exhaustive inventory of items to select from. By 'processing' a given learner through the model one ends up with a fairly complete list of language forms to be produced or recognized. These can then form the basis for the construction of the syllabus.

Although intended as a syllabus design tool, Munby's model also lends itself to test design. It was used in a fairly unmodified form as the starting point for design of the ELTS test. In Figure 2.10 we looked briefly at part of the criterion performance of a post-graduate student at a British university. This has been broken down into Events and Activities and one activity has been analysed by specifying a number of extracts from Munby's inventory of language skills deemed to be relevant to *intensive reading for academic purposes*. A similar procedure with the other activities will yield a complete list of relevant language skills. These can then be sampled at the next stage of test construction, to provide the test proficiency.

Brilliant though it is as a work of synthesis, the very completeness of Munby's model makes it rather cumbersome to use in practice. Some of the psychosocial parameters seem too delicate to be relevant to practical teaching and testing concerns. There is also an uneasy indeterminacy between the social and behavioural parameters and their linguistic realizations. Vocabulary size and range, for example, is not easily constrained by the model. Nevertheless, Munby's work has provided an invaluable aid to syllabus and test designers, and 'stripped-down' versions have been adopted by several testing bodies.

**Difficulties with the analysis of the criterion performance**
A fair amount of information about the learner is required in order to carry out the
kind of analysis described above. This information can be obtained in two ways.

1 Detailed observation of individuals in some occupational or social setting. This
has the advantage of giving reliable information but is very time-consuming and
requires specially trained personnel.

2. Imaginative speculation by the designer about the learner's activities and the
demands made on his language skills. This is clearly quicker and easier but if the
imaginary information is grossly distorted or incomplete, then the best analysis in
the world is not going to yield a relevant criterion proficiency. The tendency here is
to produce descriptions of stereotypes, performances of 'typical' waiters, etc. which
may not conform very closely to the reality of the learners' future activities. Unfortunately many of the inputs to the ELTS blueprint were fictitious in this sense and this
has attracted criticism. Clearly where direct observation is not feasible it is important
that speculative description be based upon informed sources.

## 6.3.2  Sampling the criterion proficiency

The inventory of enabling skills and functions which a complete analysis of the
criterion performance can produce may be very large. In the case of the ELTS test,
when the criterion performance is the complex business of studying at a university,
the specification can be very detailed indeed. This inventory must clearly be
sampled in order to obtain a managable sub-set for test construction purposes. As
mentioned in section 2.2.2. the temptation only to choose those aspects of the
proficiency which can be most easily incorporated into the test design should be
recognized and if possible avoided. Thus it may be easier to establish through an
indirect test whether a candidate can 'interpret' or 'substantiate' than it is to assess
ability to 'thank' or 'acknowledge'. Nevertheless the latter functions may form an
equally or more important part of the criterion proficiency. Administrative constraints may inevitably distort sampling but it is better if this is explicitly recognized
rather than simply being allowed to happen.

## 6.3.3 Test construction

The next stage involves the devising of a series of tasks which will allow the
candidate to demonstrate the extent to which he possesses the test proficiency. At
this stage the test designer will be constrained by administrative matters and his
choice of format will be guided by two conflicting considerations: while the test must
mobilize the skills and knowledge which make up the test proficiency it must also be
easy to administer and score. Multiple-choice and gap-filling test formats satisfy the
latter requirement though, as we saw earlier (3.3.2), the lack of real-time constraints
during pencil-and-paper tests make extrapolation to time-constrained performances rather an inexact business. For this reason such formats are probably better
used for tests where the criterion performance is not very time-constrained anyway
(reading tasks, writing tasks, study and reference activities) or where a time con-
straint can be introduced into the test (e.g. listening tests based on taped materials).

## 6.3.4  Measurement and judgement

The last job of the test designer is deciding on a scoring system and a pass-mark or other basis for judgement. The close-endedness of the indirect-item type makes measurement fairly easy: one simply counts the number of correct responses. Unlike the direct test there is no problem with inter-scorer reliability.

The difficulties arise with the judgement stage where a meaning must be given to the scores. Since what the candidate has to do in the test is quite different from the criterion performance, mere inspection of the test is not usually enough to decide what constitutes a satisfactory score. Some kind of empirical validation is necessary, preferably using a more direct test based on a similar criterion performance.

Carroll (1980) proposes a procedure for converting indirect test scores to equivalent performance bands using a kind of empirical method.

Where a group of candidates takes some kind of direct test such as an oral production test which is scored using a band descriptor system described earlier, these scores can be used to calibrate an indirect test (say, a listening test) administered to the same candidates.

A sample of candidates from across the range of scores on the indirect test is drawn at intervals of ten percentiles. Thus if 50 candidates take the test, the first, fifth, tenth, etc. candidates are chosen. A graph is drawn with the listening test scores on one axis and the oral bands on the other. Points are plotted for each sample candidate corresponding to his listening and oral scores (see Fig. 6.9). These are then joined by a curve of 'best fit'.

From now on the listening score of any candidate can be converted into a band score by reading off the relevant intercept on the curve. Conversely, if we decide for example that an oral performance score of 6.5 is the minimum satisfactory for a particular purpose, then the 'pass-mark' on the listening test can be read off the curve as 67.

An immediate objection can be made to this procedure on the grounds that the criterion performances for each test are quite different, one being a test of oral production and the other of listening and it is therefore inappropriate to calibrate one against the other. This is defended (Carroll and Hall, 1985) by saying that 'broadly speaking . . . a person who speaks well can also listen well'. Implausible though this justification is, the procedure is undoubtedly better than one alternative, which is to arbitrarily assign grades and pass-marks to the listening-test scores without reference to any external criterion. In the absence of other ways of giving meaning to scores it is certainly better than nothing.

## 6.3.5  Indirect tests – advantages and drawbacks

As we have seen then, almost every part of the test construction process has some problem associated with it. The overall effect of these problems is to reduce the degree of confidence with which decisions can be based on test results, i.e. to threaten the validity of the test in the broadest sense of the word. Inadequacies in the analysis used to derive the criterion proficiency from the criterion performance affect the construct validity of the test so that it may fail to be a proper specification of the necessary knowledge and skills.

Distortions of sampling brought about by administrative constraints threaten the

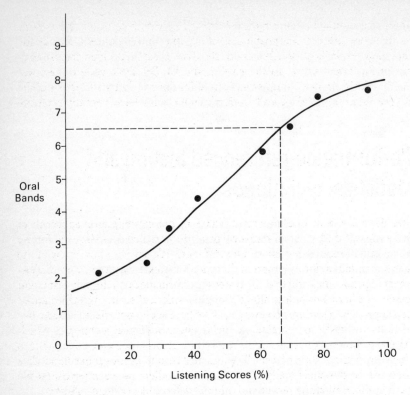

Fig 6.9

content validity of the test so that even if the analysis is adequate, the sample which is chosen for testing may not be representative. Finally, the whole question of the meaning of the scores is made indeterminate by the dissimilarity between test and criterion performances.

In spite of these formidable drawbacks, indirect tests are the rule rather than the exception in most testing situations. There are two reasons for this. The first concerns ease of administration. A direct test is extremely costly in terms of time and personnel. Often only one candidate can be tested at a time and assessors must be specially trained. A 'paper-and-pencil' test, on the other hand, can be taken by a large number of candidates at the same time and can be administered by relatively untrained personnel. Scoring can be done at a later stage, again by untrained personnel if the questions are of the closed-response type.

In many situations, testing could not take place at all if advantage were not taken of these aspects of indirect test types.

The second consideration is that of reliability. While there are certainly other sources of unreliability than inter-scorer variations, the elimination of this source by using closed-response items can make a big difference to the robustness of the test instrument.

These two gains, in ease of administration and reliability, make the indirect approach to testing the natural choice particularly for large-scale testing programmes at a national or international level. The extent to which these gains outweigh the concomitant compromising of validity and indeterminacy in the interpretation of results is obviously something which must be decided according to the merits of individual cases. In the case of the ELTS test a compromise was reached in that fairly direct techniques were used for the oral and written parts of the test while the listening, reading and study-skills modules have a multiple-choice format.

# 6.4 Performance-referenced testing and statistical techniques

In Chapter 4 we saw how one important legacy of the psychometric approach to language testing was the battery of statistical procedures which could be used for the development and monitoring of the test instruments. We saw also how many of the techniques depended on the assumption that each sub-test measured a one-dimensional aspect of proficiency and that the testees' performances on the sub-test could be expressed as a series of points along a single numerical scale. A performance-referenced approach to testing, however, is, as we have seen, more likely to make use of *lists* of skills and tasks to characterize proficiency. Statistical techniques which assume that one-dimensional 'strengths' underlie performance may be difficult to apply coherently to these sorts of tests. Treating test results as one-dimensional data for the purpose of statistical analysis can lead to conflicts between psychometric virtues such as discriminating power and other *desiderata* like content validity.

Does this mean, then, that the performance-referenced test designer must approach the task of test development unarmed, statistically speaking? Not necessarily. As we shall see, many of the psychometrician's techniques can be adapted to the purpose of developing performance-referenced tests. Others turn out to be unnecessary since they were developed to solve problems that do not arise with performance-referenced tests.

## 6.4.1 Direct tests

In general direct tests require less statistical massaging during their development than indirect tests. Much statistical work involves establishing how difficult a test is (with respect to some population) and what the pass-mark should be. A direct test, as we have seen, can be inspected to see how difficult it is and inspection and consultation with informers is usually sufficient to decide what sort of performance is satisfactory. At the same time direct tests are not usually made of independent ('discrete') sub-tasks, so that item-analysis and sub-test weighting are not appropriate techniques. For these reasons the problems involved in developing direct tests (finding tasks that elicit a suitable performance, refining band descriptors, etc.) do not require much in the way of statistical analysis.

The exception to this is the measurement of inter-assessor reliability (see 4.6.6). As noted earlier, when an assessment is made of a complex performance, there is always the possibility of variability in the assessors' judgement. One way of finding out how big a problem this is is to have each performance assessed by two independent assessors. A correlation coefficient can be calculated between the two sets of scores. Although the interpretation of this value, like that of any correlation coefficient, is a risky business, if the value is less than about 0.7 then the assessors, their training or the band descriptors probably need looking at.

## 6.4.2  Indirect tests

In the case of indirect tests, decisions have to be made such as how difficult the test is, and what the pass-mark should be, which can't be made by merely inspecting the test construction procedure because of the dissimilarity between test and criterion performances. Such decisions can be made more easily and with greater confidence using information which statistical analysis can yield about the behaviour of the test and its parts. A listening test which gives a mean result of 28 per cent when administered to a group whose listening abilities are judged to be in the range of 'adequate' (for the purpose of the criterion performance) is clearly too difficult. Perhaps the instructions were not clear or the content of the listening material was obscure but, whatever the reason, the low mean reveals some deficiency in the test design.

The use of ranking statistics, percentiles, etc. to assign grades and passes (as outlined in 4.4) is not really appropriate in performance-referenced testing. Establishing what the pass-mark should be in a multiple-choice listening test is best done by empirical means. Even the rather suspect procedure described in 6.3.4 is better than deciding to award grades and passes to arbitarily chosen percentile slices of the test population. The ideal solution would be to construct a more direct test based on the criterion performance (note-taking for instance) and use a graphical method to calibrate the multiple-choice test against this. Subsequent versions of the test could be norm-referenced if the ability level of the population were stable enough, though this would only ensure equivalence of difficulty between versions rather than equivalence of *domain*. To make sure that the test results continued to reflect the criterion performance (i.e. note-taking ability) we would have to repeat the validation for each new version of the multiple-choice test. For this kind of validation we can use the graphical method described above and also look at the correlation coefficient, though as always, the value of this index is not particularly informative in itself.

Item analysis is another technique which can be used with the performance-referenced test though the unidimensional trait assumptions underlying their use should make us careful about following their indications to the letter. Indices of difficulty or discrimination can point to items which are too difficult or easy or fail to discriminate because of some overlooked flaw in construction such as implausible distractors or hidden tricks, etc. What needs to be resisted is the rejection of an item on purely statistical grounds even if there appears to be nothing wrong with its construction. As long as the correct response requires application of a relevant part of the test proficiency then there is no reason to reject it.

A variation of the discrimination index can be useful for developing performance-referenced tests. Instead of using the scores on the test itself to identify the low and high scoring groups for the analysis, the groups can be constituted on the basis of the candidates' scores on a more direct test. In this way the items selected as being good discriminators are those which discriminate between performance according to a meaningful criterion. This practice still subscribes to the idea of a unidimensional trait underlying the performance but in this case at least, the trait is linked to a relevant criterion. The method (described and illustrated in Carroll and Hall, 1984) is a good example of a statistical technique which can be adapted for the development of non-psychometric tests without introducing conflicts in underlying assumptions and principles.

It is clear then that the performance-referenced test designer does have a repertoire of useful statistical techniques. One point emerges during the brief survey above: those procedures which prove most useful are those which can be used in establishing relationships between direct and indirect tests, i.e. giving meaning to the content and results of indirect tests by linking them to some meaningful criterion. The techniques which assist this work of validation and calibration are valuable tools for the test designer. Those techniques, on the other hand, which evaluate test and item behaviour in a vacuum without reference to domain or performance are not really appropriate to the development of these kinds of test.

# 7

# Test purpose and test type

In the last few chapters we have been examining approaches to testing on the basis of the criterion used and its relationship to the test performance. now we have to relate these test types to the variety of purposes for which tests are required.

## 7.1 Identifying decisions

At the beginning of the book we established that the purpose of a test is to arrive at a decision. Procedures which do not lead to decisions of any kind are not really tests in the strict sense; rather different principles apply to their construction from those relevant to tests proper. Nevertheless, such 'ceremonies' and 'goads', as we called them in Chapter 1, may have an important function to fulfil. The 'washback' effect, whereby the nature of the exit test for an instructional course influences the teaching leading up to it, is well known. It may have a harmful influence on teaching: indirect tests which involve candidates in rather unnatural activities such as multiple-choice tests may lead to excessive practice of these activities in the classroom, bringing little benefit to the learners. A performance-referenced or task-based test, however, may have a beneficial influence on previously rather passive instructional regimes by encouraging teachers to use more active kinds of practice activities.

Within national educational systems this effect can be exploited to bring about curriculum reform. By changing the exam which the learners must pass at the end of their courses one may influence course content and methodology more effectively than by issuing ministerial directives to administrators and teachers. The method needs to be used with discretion however, and due consideration given to teachers' flexibility and its limitations.

Leaving aside this role of tests as curriculum modifiers, we will concentrate on the decision-facilitating function of language testing. A survey of test purpose, then, is a matter of identifying the points at which decisions need to be made within educational and occupational contexts.

We can usefully distinguish between tests which are created for use within some programme of language instruction and 'public' language examinations which are directed at a wider audience.

# 7.2 Testing within language instruction programmes

All instructional programmes need a way of deciding who to admit to the programme, monitoring performance and evaluating the outcome. Tests to provide information for these decisions we can call entrance, progress and exit tests.

## 7.2.1 Entrance tests

### Multi-level, non-ESP programmes

Where an institution offers general language courses for learners at a variety of 'levels', the entrance or placement test indicates in which of the available groups a learner will learn most effectively. Reasons of economy usually dictate that teaching groups be larger than two or three and in order to use the teacher's time most effectively it is desirable that the learners' response to the activities should be as similar as possible, in other words that the group should be 'homogeneous'. If this is not the case then the amount of individual attention required by each learner exceeds the teacher's resources and the group cannot be taught effectively. The larger the group, the more important that it be homogeneous in this sense.

Two factors contribute to the homogeneity of a language class. One concerns the size of the learners 'repertoire' and the other the extent of development of ancillary skills.

A group of learners can be taught most effectively together if they have the same degree of familiarity (or unfamiliarity) with the material which will form the content of the course. Within limits the exact degree is not so important. Providing the time required to master the material is roughly the same for each learner then they can move through the course together.

Another way in which the learners must be similar is in terms of the ancillary skills and knowledge which they need to participate in the course. Where the teaching is done in the medium of the target language a certain level of listening ability is required to enable the learner to follow instructions. If the course involves reading or writing activities, script recognition and production skills will be required. Again the exact level of these abilities is not as important as that they should be developed to a similar degree in all the members of the group.

Ideally, then, an entrance test to a multi-level programme should give information about the degree of familiarity of the learner with the content envisaged for the courses as well as assessing the mastery of the necessary ancillary skills.

To probe familiarity with the content of the courses an indirect test is indicated for ease of administration and marking: The criterion proficiency used as the basis for the course syllabus may be sampled to provide the test proficiency. A test can then be written using the usual indirect formats, multiple-choice, sentence completion, etc.

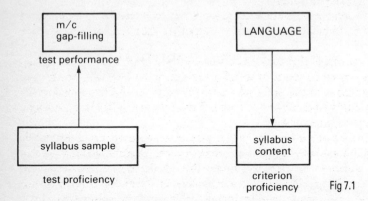

Fig 7.1

To provide information about enabling skills, listening and reading tests can be prepared based on the criterion performance of 'participating in a language class':

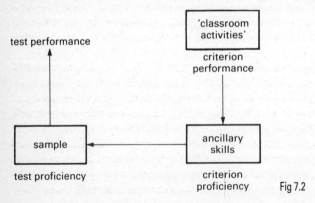

Fig 7.2

A fully-fledged test specification to provide this information would be very elaborate. In practice, however, such sophistication is often unnecessary. Where the number of levels is limited it is pointless to administer a test of great length or complexity in order to choose between such a small number of alternatives. Where there are only three or four different levels, a thirty-item multiple-choice grammar test is usually sufficient while a cloze test based on a text of suitable difficulty will often give a satisfactory spread (see section 5.4). Time and personnel are often at a premium and results are usually required quickly for placement purposes. For these reasons an entrance test should give the necessary information as economically as possible.

Standard psychometric techniques can be used for the development of such tests since, by using a series of levels for the programme, we are already subscribing to the convenient fiction that language proficiency is a one-dimensional construct. Thus the use of standard deviations to choose between prospective tests and the use of item analysis is in keeping with the aims for which the test is being developed. If time permits, a short interview can be used to assess the candidate's oral/aural abilities.

### One-off and ESP programmes

When the decision to be made is not *which* group a learner should be admitted to but *whether* he should be admitted to a particular course then the role of the entrance test is different.

Such courses are often ESP courses developed for a specific group of learners and the job of the entrance test is to indicate the degree to which the prospective participants have mastered the prerequisite knowledge and abilities to follow the course. Courses of this kind can be so various that it is better to look at an example rather than attempt to generalize.

Let us take the case of a course in interdepartmental report-writing for middle managers of a multinational corporation. Analysis of the report-writing tasks that the participants will have to carry out reveal that all the time available will be required to practise the specific micro-features associated with this kind of writing as well as the rhetorical-organizational principles which must be grasped in order to write an effective report. There will be little time available for 'remedial' work on more general aspects of the language system. For this reason, only those candidates who can already demonstrate a mastery of basic syntactic and organizational features in writing can be admitted to the course. The function of the entrance test then, would be to indicate to what extent prospective participants already have control of these features.

If time and staff are in short supply then a standard multiple-choice grammar test could be used to assess candidates' suitability. This would have two drawbacks, however. Firstly the test would give no information about the candidates' ability to mobilize the features during an actual writing performance. Secondly the setting of the pass-mark for the test would have to be a fairly arbitrary business. A more appropriate format for the entrance test would be a more direct test based on a series of writing tasks and scores according to a band-descriptor scale. The more important the success of the course and the more valuable the time of the participants, the more trouble it is worth taking to ensure that the entrance test really does select those who are in a position to benefit from the course.

## 7.2.2 Progress tests

Although, as we have seen, the progress test is frequently used as a goad to encourage application on the part of the learners, it can in theory serve as a basis for decisions about course content, learner placement and future course design.

The results of a progress test can be used as a pointer to parts of the course content which have not been mastered by significant numbers of learners and thus to indicate need for remedial action. The information provided by the test to teachers and course designers will be more useful if the test is of the indirect type. This is because it is easier to identify which aspects of the course content are giving problems if this is broken down into small items, whereas a failure to perform well in a direct test could be due to weakness in a variety of different areas. An indirect test is more useful for these 'diagnostic' purposes. A properly written progress test sampling correctly from the course content can be an indication to learners which part of the course need more attention, and to course designers which parts of the course have not been effective.

Such tests are among the easiest to prepare since the analysis of the criterion has already been done by the course designer in order to decide the course content. All the test constructor has to do is to sample from this proficiency and devise a test to measure it.

## 7.2.3  Exit tests

Most courses of language instruction end with an exit test of some kind. The role and form of the test depend upon whether the course is a general language course or whether it was designed to prepare learners for some specific future goal, i.e. an ESP course.

### General courses

As with progress tests, we have seen that exit tests too can be entirely devoid of decision-making purpose, i.e. when they are merely an end-of-course ritual. In the case of general language courses this state of affairs is more the rule than the exception. Since the course is not intended to prepare the learner for any specific future performance, the only decision that the exit test can facilitate is the relatively trivial one of whether to award a certificate or not.

The procedure for constructing an exit test for a general language course is as straightforward as that for making a progress test. The syllabus designer has already performed the analysis which identifies the criterion proficiency. The test constructor merely has to sample this proficiency and construct a test to measure it. Setting grades and pass-marks may be a problem since there is no criterion performance, but the procedure described in section 4.3.4 for calibrating the test against the teachers' impressions of learner performance may be used.

There is one case in which the exit test of a general language course can serve as a basis for an important decision and that is when the exit test for one course serves as the entrance test for the next. In this case it is the responsibility of the course designer to ensure that the level reached at the end of one course satisfies the prerequisites for the course above. It is not unusual in language teaching institutions to find that learners who have moved up through the levels are at a disadvantage with respect to 'new' students from outside who have been placed in the same classes using the entrance test. When this happens either the entrance test or the course design needs to be revised.

### Exit tests from ESP courses

In an ESP course the content will have been wholly or partly derived from a consideration of some future task which the learners will have to carry out using the target language. For the sake of consistency it is desirable that the same performance specification which is used for the course design should also constitute the criterion performance which the design of the exit test takes as its starting point.

In view of what has been said about the validity of direct and indirect tests, it should be clear that the exit test of an ESP course should be as direct as administrative constraints will allow. Thus, in the case of the report-writing course mentioned earlier, the best exit test would be to have the participants actually write a report using information from a source-file. In this way, providing the test and assessment procedures have been carried out properly, we get a clear answer to the question 'This candidate has finished the course. Now, can he really write a report?'

Where the criterion performance is less easily simulatable or resources are limited we may have to resort to indirect testing, at least for part of a test. We can try and minimize the effect this will have on validity by using indirect procedures only for assessing non-time-constrained aspects of the performance such as reading, etc. In general, though, the most appropriate procedure will be a direct one and will have an additional beneficial effect on teaching by focusing the attention of teachers and learners on the concrete goals of the instruction.

# 7.3 Public language examinations

So far we have been looking at tests which are designed to fulfil a particular function within a language teaching programme. Tests produced by public bodies (which we will call examinations) are not generally produced with any particular course of instruction in mind (although they may be used as exit or entrance tests for courses within institutions). These tests depend for their survival on finding a wide enough fee-paying audience to cover the costs of developing and administering the exam. For this reason such exams in the past have been almost exclusively of a system-referenced type in order that they should be relevant to as wide a range of users as possible. 'Recognition' of an exam occurs when the associated certificate is accepted as an indication of capacity to produce a performance which is of interest to some decision-making body. Thus the Cambridge Syndicate's Proficiency examination is accepted as a qualification for teachers of English in the state schools of some European countries. As we have seen (see 2.3.2), a system-referenced exam can be linked to a performance only in an informal way. Such recognition takes a long time to achieve and often bears little relation to the real value of the exam. Thus the language laboratory-based exams produced by the ARELS organization have received little recognition inside or outside Britain, in spite of being some of the most effective measures of general oral proficiency currently available.

Although an examination may not achieve recognition in the above sense it may still find a market among teaching institutions that wish to use it as an exit test for their courses. In this way the work of course design is made easier since the syllabus content will be drawn from the criterion proficiency on which the exam is based. The prospect of the exam at the end of term also gives direction and motivation to the endeavours of teachers and learners. In addition, the staff are saved the trouble of devising and administering an exit test for the course. Although the decision-making function of an exam used in this way is minimal (unless a pass is needed to enter a subsequent course) its 'ritual' importance should not be underestimated. When choosing a public exam for this purpose, the user should examine the content carefully to check that the criterion proficiency covers areas which will be useful or relevant to the learners and that the inevitable 'washback' effect of teachers teaching for the exam will lead to classroom activities which are in line with the pedagogic approach of the institution. An exam which encourages teachers to spend the last three months of the course practising multiple-choice vocabulary items, for example, might be rejected as deleterious to the interests of the learners.

### 7.3.1  Task-based public examinations

Performance-referenced public exams tend to be fairly rare. The reasons for this are not hard to find. To justify the expense of developing a public exam, the potential audience should be as large as possible. An exam which is based upon one particular performance is unlikely to be viable in this respect. The exceptions to this are the British Council ELTS test and other exams used for university entrance purposes. In this case the audience, although specific, has grown so much in recent years as to constitute a reasonable market.

Although the need for generality has prevented the development of truly per-formance-referenced public exams, the last few years have seen the emergence of a number of examinations based upon test performances very similar to actual language use. These cannot be regarded as performance-referenced in the strict sense because, although they may involve doing things like reading tourist informa-tion, listening to radio advertisements, etc., they are not intended to give specific information about a candidate's ability to do these things. They should be regarded as **task-based** tests in the sense explained in Chapter 6. Their function is the same as that of the more traditional examinations looked at earlier, i.e. to give direction and content to a course of language instruction. Their emergence can be seen as a response to dissatisfaction on the part of teaching institutions in Britain and elsewhere with more traditional public exams. Changing emphasis in classroom methodology towards more realistic language practice did not square well with the methods required to prepare learners for very indirect system-referenced tests. This had the effect of creating a potential market for more direct exams with a more acceptable 'washback' effect. The result was the development in Britain of a number of task-based exams by bodies such as the Royal Society of Arts and the Oxford Syndicate. At the same time other examining bodies have made modifications to their existing exams by incorporating more task-based sub-tests.

# 7.4  Deciding to test – seven key questions

Testing has become an unavoidable part of the business of language instruction. Some of the reasons for this are good ones: teachers, learners and administrators all need information, motivation and reassurance from time to time and tests can provide this. At the same time, the testing which takes place for these purposes may often be unnecessary, inappropriate, misleading, harmful and unhelpful in a dozen different ways. These undesirable effects are usually the result of regarding the test procedures as ends in themselves, rather than instrumental to the achievement of some goal. This trap can be avoided by establishing *why* a test is necessary before anything else is considered. Once this is done the selection of an appropriate procedure follows easily and naturally.

We can make this selection process explicit by answering a series of questions about the test context:

**1 Will a decision follow from the results of this test?**

If the answer is 'no', the next question must be:

**2. Is a test necessary then?**

If the answer is 'yes' ('The students won't study otherwise', 'The principal says all courses have to finish with a test') then the test procedure merely has to look enough like a test to motivate the students or satisfy the principal; if the answer is 'no' then we have saved time and trouble.

If the answer to question 1 is 'yes', a decision will follow' then we embark on the business of selection.

**3. What is the decision?**

**4. What information do we need in order to make it?**

If we have to decide whether to admit candidates to an MBA course, for example, then the information we need to know is whether their language abilities are equal to the demands which the course will make on them.

**5. Is there an acceptable (feasible, affordable) test already in existence which will provide this information?**

If the answer is 'yes' then our job is finished. If not, then we will have to prepare the test ourselves.

**6. What procedure would give us this information to an adequate degree of accuracy and completeness?**

If the decision is a relatively unimportant one we will be looking for an economical test procedure. If, on the other hand, mistakes would be costly, we will want to base it on very reliable information. In the case of the MBA candidates we would ideally want to simulate a wide range of the course activities. Before getting carried away we must move quickly to the last question:

**7. What time, personnel and resources are available for planning, piloting, administering and monitoring this procedure?**

When we have answered the last two questions we are in a position to start planning the test. Depending upon these answers our design will be more or less elaborate.

Of the above questions all but number 6 can be answered by looking carefully at the educational or occupational context. A satisfactory answer to question 6 demands an understanding of the range of procedures available to the language tester and their relationship to the decision-making which lies at the root of the testing process. It has been the purpose of this book to enable the reader to arrive at a clear, coherent answer to that question.

# References

CAROLL, B. J. 1980: *Testing communicative performance: an interim study.* Oxford: Pergamon

CARROLL, B. J. and HALL, P. J. 1985: *Make your own language tests: a practical guide to writing language performance tests.* Oxford: PERGAMON.

CAROLL, J. B. 1961: Fundamental considerations in testing for English proficiency of foreign students. In Allen, H. B. and Campbell, R. N. (eds.) 1972: *Teaching English as a foreign language: a book of readings.* New York: McGraw Hill.

GOFFMAN, I. 1959: *The presentation of self in everyday life.* Harmondsworth: Penguin.

HALLIDAY, M. A. K. 1973: *Explorations in the functions of language.* London: Edward Arnold.

HUGHES, A. and PORTER, D. (ed.) 1983: *Current developments in language testing.* London: Academic Press.

LADO, R. 1961: *Language testing.* London: Longman.

MUNBY, J. 1978: *Communicative syllabus design.* Cambridge: CUP.

OLLER, J. 1979: *Language tests at school.* London: Longman.

OLLER, J. (ed.) 1983: *Issues in language testing research.* Cambridge, Mass.: Newbury House.

PALMER, A. S. and BACHMAN, L. F. 1980: Basic concerns in test validation. In Alderson, J. and Hughes, A. (eds.) 1981: *Issues in Language testing.* British Council ELT Documents 111.

SANG, F. SCHMITZ, B. VOLLMER, H. J. BEAUMERT, J. and ROEDER, P. M. 1986: Models of second language competence: a structural equation approach. In *Language Testing* 3, 39–53.

VAN EK, J. 1975: *The threshold level.* Strasbourg: Council of Europe.

# Further Reading

## 1 Handbooks

HEATON, J. B. 1975: *Writing English language tests.* London: Longman.
Survey of the testing techniques available at the beginning of the 1970s. Many practical examples.

VALLETTE, R. M. 1977: *Modern language testing.* New York: Harcourt Brace Jovanovich. Highly eclectic collection of (mostly) classroom testing techniques.

CARROLL, B. J. and HALL, P. J. 1985: *Make your own language tests: a practical guide to writing language performance tests.* Oxford: Pergamon. More amply illustrated and accessible presentation of ideas from Carroll's earlier book (see below).

## 2 Theoretical Texts

LADO, R. 1961: *Language testing.* London: Longman. Seminal work by one of the founders of modern language testing.

ALLEN, J. and DAVIES, A. (eds.) 1977: *Testing and experimental methods.* The Edinburgh course in applied linguistics. OUP. Good overview of the position in the mid-1970s

CARROLL, B. J. 1980: *Testing communicative performance: an interim study.* Oxford: Pergamon. Important exposition of the principles of performance-referenced testing.

HENNING, G. 1987: *Language testing: development, evaluation, research.* Cambridge, Mass.: Newbury House. Up-to-date account of psychometric testing. Thorough treatment of statistical techniques.

## 3 Collections of papers

OLLER, J. and PERKINS, K. (eds.) 1980: *Research in language testing.* Rowley, Mass.: Newbury house. Research into 'pragmatic' testing techniques.

OLLER, J. (ed.) 1983: *Issues in language testing research.* Rowley, Mass.: Newbury House.

HUGHES, A. and PORTER, D. (ed.) 1983: *Current developments in language testing.* London: Academic Press. Discussion of the 'Unitary Competence Hypothesis'.

ALDERSON, J. C. and HUGHES, A. (eds.) 1981: *Issues in Language testing.* British Council ELT Documents 111. Reports of seminars on three key areas of controversy in language testing.

# INDEX